VICTORY IN THE WAIT

Victory in the Wait

My Journey to Unwavering Faith

†

Sylvester Baugh

InsideOut Press
PO Box 2666
Country Club Hills, IL 60478

Copyright © 2022 by Sylvester Baugh

All rights reserved. No part of this book may be reproduced in any form on by an electronic or mechanical means, including information storage and retrieval systems, without permission in writing from the publisher, except by a reviewer who may quote brief passages in a review.

First edition July 2022

Cover design by Denise Daub
Interior design by Veronica Daub

For more information about publishing services, please visit www.InsideOutPress.com.

Printed in the United States of America

Library of Congress Control Number: 2022911958

ISBN- 978-0-9992111-9-9

This book is dedicated to my family, friends, church family, and medical staff. Thank you for supporting me on my journey. Genuine love, care, prayer, and support are vitally important when in a season of wait and I am forever grateful that my support system demonstrated these characteristics. To my granddaughters, Leilani, Linae, and Leah. You are truly my angels and I love you dearly.

Foreword

One of the toughest things to do in life is wait. I must confess that patience is not one of my greatest attributes, yet I have learned that there are certain things in life that are worth waiting for. Before my beautiful wife finally accepted my proposal to marry her, she rejected me at least six times. However, since she has said "yes," it has been the best thing that has ever happened to me. Even as it relates to my relationship with God, I have learned that there is a blessing in waiting on the Lord. Waiting on God helps us trust Him more. At the end of the day, as believers, we must trust God's will for our lives. We must believe in His timing and know that whatever God has for us, He will give it to us when He knows we are ready to receive it. I truly believe that the best way to overcome this world, with all its trials and tribulations, is by learning the power of waiting on God.

When I think about Sylvester, the first word that comes to my mind is "overcomer." Over the past couple of years, as Sylvester's spiritual leader, I have personally seen the struggles he has faced with his health. However, because he is an overcomer, I have also witnessed his resilience and his refusal to give in to his physical ailments. This is why I feel Sylvester's most recent literary work, Victory in the Wait, is a must read. Within this book, you will read about Sylvester's journey from sickness to wholeness through his willingness to wait on God. At the same time, he will provide you strategies on how to patiently wait on God without allowing bitterness and resentment to build up within your soul. Sylvester is a living testament that great things come to those who wait.

So, as you get ready to read this book, be ready to be inspired and motivated to push through all your struggles and setbacks, in order to attain the victory God has for you. Learn from Sylvester's journey and allow his story to encourage you to wait on God even when you feel like you have been forgotten by God. I truly believe your life is about to change as you learn about the Victory in the Wait.

– Pastor Moses B. Herring, Sr.
Senior Pastor of Faith Movers Church

Chapter One

*"Wait on the Lord, be of good courage,
and He shall strengthen thine heart.
Wait, I say, on the Lord."*
– Psalm 27:14

Our lives are full of waiting. We wait for phone calls, lab results, and ride-share service. The real difference lies in how we handle the waiting.

For many of us, waiting for relief from the unknown is often accompanied by weight—the weight of stress, the weight of anxiety, the weight of impatience. We all know that waiting demands our attention, and the required patience is a critical skill we learn in life. So, why is it so difficult? To wait means to stay, standstill, or delay a particular reaction until a certain time or event occurs. Psalm 27:14 suggests that in our waiting, we should be able to avoid the weight: "Wait on the Lord, be of good courage." Courage suggests the ability to face something that can cause grief or pain. No wonder waiting is such a challenge—facing pain or grief usually comes with the "F" word: fear.

Fear is a natural and widely understood response. However, in our voyage through faith, we are not encouraged to embrace fear or rely on our own human wisdom. So, what are we to do? "Without faith, it is impossible to please God" (Hebrews 11:6 New Living Translation).

I thought I could demonstrate "unwavering faith" if I did not have to find courage while waiting, but therein lies our problem. I have talked to many people who have struggled in this area, and some are unaware that they are struggling. Having had first-hand experience with the struggle, I understand. But if I had to do it all over again, I would not change a thing. At first, I did not understand that God is the ultimate tactician. Now, I know that every aspect of every component in all that I experienced was designed to prepare me for greater faith development. It was a plan to teach me things I otherwise may not have ever learned.

I can say that I am very familiar with this process of waiting. I wish I could tell you it was easy and that my journey was unblemished, but I cannot. I experienced negative thoughts and challenging responses, and there were times I wanted to give up. I am only human, and every person has a breaking point. I believed that if I just gave up, people would understand. I had lived a decent life, and what was facing me seemed exceedingly difficult. These are moments that I never shared with anyone.

For most of my life, I have relied on my own intelligence or wisdom to help me manage challenging situations. I have used these gifts to encourage others, as well as manage my life. When I was faced with this unfamiliar situation, one I was unprepared for, the moments of stress, confusion, and anxiety began to weigh on me. The weight pulled me down to an incredibly low point in my life. When I faced the wait, my resolve to fight became stronger, and I did the only thing I could do. What follows is my story.

Chapter Two

*"The mind of a man plans his way,
but the Lord directs his steps."*
– Proverbs 16:9

My story begins in 2010. My wife and I had just purchased a new home, and we were looking forward to doing some wonderful things. What I looked most forward to was identifying a new church home. I left my former church about two to three years before moving because my pastor decided to retire. Being void of a spiritual covering was not comfortable for me, so I was searching and wondering where I would go next.

I began a season of waiting.

I waited for God to lead me to the right church so that my family and I would have our spiritual covering. During my season of waiting, my sister told me about a church she enjoyed attending. I hoped it would be the church that would end my waiting season, but when I visited, something just did not feel right. I enjoyed the preacher teaching the Word, but I didn't feel the warmth of the congregation. That was important to me. After a few weeks, I stopped attending on Sundays and started to attend the weekly Bible study on Wednesdays. I believed that receiving the message from this awesome preacher with a smaller gathering of people might be a better experience.

I began to enjoy myself, feeling a connection to this pastor. His messages were so relevant and moving that I went to listen regularly; I never wanted to miss it. After a few months of attending, I began to feel conflicted. On the one hand, I felt that this pastor was someone I could learn from and grow with. On the other hand, I still didn't feel a connection with the congregation. I did not feel welcomed, and I wondered if it was just me. Was I being too sensitive? Was I expecting too much? Had I been spoiled by my previous church? I was so confused, but I prayed and continued to try to figure this out on my own. As time went by, I began to think that maybe I would just continue going to Bible study. I still felt that it was important for me, my wife, and our two daughters to have a spiritual covering. During that time of indecision, I recalled sharing a hypothetical with a fellow member who was also a member of my former church: If only I could find a way to get our previous, retired pastor and this current pastor in one church, operating in ministry together. I knew that this idea was a long shot, but a guy can dream, can't he?

Now, I have heard messages about "nothing is too hard for God" and "you have not because you ask not," but in this situation, one pastor had just retired and the other was new to the church. I figured it was highly unlikely these two Mighty Men of God would ever come together. I decided to pray about it anyway. A new season of waiting began.

As the weeks went by, I shared my prayer with others and found people who agreed with me. I began to feel that maybe this union was not such a crazy idea after all, but I never developed any faith that it would happen. I just liked the fact that others agreed with me. So, while I waited, I never believed. I never had faith.

"Faith is the substance of things hoped for and the evidence of things not seen" (Hebrews 11:1). I never believed my fantasy could happen. If you do not believe, your wait is devoid of faith. I felt in my spirit that I needed to see some evidence that this union was possible. If you feel that you need to see evidence, faith is not present. I thought I had faith, but I had more doubt than faith. I was beginning to feel the "weight" of my wait.

As I mentioned previously, throughout a season of waiting, the weight can come in many forms. Often, the weight is manifested by a variety of emotions: anger, fear, frustration, disappointment, confusion, etc. While continuing to attend bible study and wishing for this unlikely union, I began to feel some of those emotions, particularly frustration and confusion.

"For God is not the author of confusion, but of peace, as in all churches of the saints" (Corinthians 14:33). Peace? I did not see or feel peace in this new church, and I did not feel peace in my spirit. I know what the Word said, but in this case, the Word missed the mark. Because of the inconsistency, I remained confused. When things do not line up with the way I think, I believe it deserves to be questioned. So, yes, I was questioning the Word of God. As I reflect today, I feel I could've never really been that doubtful man. Along your spiritual journey toward knowing and understanding God, how sure are you that you truly know who you are? Sure, I prayed, I encouraged people, I helped people, but is that really who I was?

At this point in my life, I had worked for 28 years for a youth service agency. I was known for my ability to help others achieve their goals. I was a husband, a father, and a man on a journey to know God better. That is how I was known, but that was not a complete description of who I was. Like everyone else, I had flaws. I began to wonder if the weight of living a lie was partly due to the flaws I swept under the rug. We tend to ignore our flaws because they do not represent us well. We may deny they exist, not look at them with a critical eye, or just get so accustomed to them that we perfect how we manage them. Being liked or accepted becomes our motivation to shy away from our authentic selves, caving into a culture that says, "Do it for the likes." We all enjoy some acknowledgment and adoration, but at what expense? I was not this self-aware back in 2010, but now that I am, I will share my story in an attempt to enlighten some and encourage others to ponder these words as it relates to their lives.

Part of my authentic self was captured in the moments I spent with my crew. These people knew a side of me that others did not. They gave me respect and kudos despite my flaws, partly because we shared many of the same flaws. These flaws became the foundation of our social construct. When I was away from my crew, I was ready to open up and face those flaws I had swept under the rug or, out of fear, kept to myself.

Have you ever been afraid of disappointing your culture? Many of us are, so we try our best to make sure that who they see results in "likes." Masking my authentic self while waiting to secure a church home was frustrating and somewhat unsettling. So, I decided I needed to have a conversation with myself.

Have you ever had moments when you wanted to face something you were dealing with and you began talking to yourself? I figured that if my culture sees all the good that I am doing for others, I could work this out for myself. In my experience, some of the most difficult conversations I have had are the ones I've had with myself. During these internal debates, my main tactics were justifying and convincing. I learned to justify who I was and ignore objective self-evaluation, the same process of recruiting or soliciting the opinions of others who you know will support your views on a matter. This can produce feelings of confidence, but does it help you get to the core of who you really are? I was convinced that I already was my authentic self, and as turns out, I was sadly mistaken.

My journey toward unwavering faith seemed too difficult of a mountain to climb. When you think about your season of waiting, what did you find most challenging? Was it patience? Was it managing your expectations? Was it the loss of control?

Throughout my season of wait, I spent time wondering why I was carrying so much weight. If you find yourself feeling the same way, ask yourself, are you being your authentic self? Are you believing in God? Through surrendering and being genuine and transparent with the Lord, you will grow closer to your authentic self. Authenticity will do two things in your life: One, you will not have to wonder who has your back; you will know. And two, you will grow exponentially as a person, spiritually.

I was not confident that I would ever have my prayers (a new church and the two mighty men of God working together) answered and I began to lose hope, but even while in the midst of my dysfunctional waiting—with fear, nonbelief, and inauthenticity—my prayers were answered.

I received a phone call, and it was from my former pastor. He asked me if I would be interested in being a part of a praise team, and I said "yes." He went on to tell me that the pastor whose church I had been attending, resigned to start a new ministry, and he wanted my former pastor to lead the music department. My former pastor happened to be an accomplished musician, writer, and producer. The joy I felt was unspeakable; God is so good! But while praising Him and celebrating, I could not help but think, did it have to take as long as it did to get us where we were now? I was quickly reminded of a scripture in Isaiah 55:8-9: "For my thoughts are not your thoughts; neither are your ways my ways." It appeared to me that I was just wasting my time, but sometimes, you need to see the entire canvas to know where improvements need to be made. God does not make mistakes. He knew what was ahead of me, but because I did not know, in my lack of faith, I just chalked it up to me being fortunate. So, I decided to just celebrate getting what I wanted and moved forward.

We were now in our new home and things were looking up. Sometimes we get so caught in external success that we fail to pay attention to what's happening internally—the development of our authentic self. My business was doing well, my family was doing well, and I was still respected and revered in many of the circles I frequented. Now that my family and I were on the verge of becoming a part of a new church, acquiring our spiritual covering, life was good. We were in position to be and do all that God wanted of us to be and to do. I felt that I had achieved my goal, but I still had issues that needed attention. So, what was next?

Chapter Three

"Be still and know that I am God."
– Psalm 46:10

A new church was formed. My new and current pastor made what he calls a "Faith Move" and left the church he was pastoring for a few years to form his own church, the Faith Movers Church (FMC). Just the name of the church alone was intriguing. We operated under the seven pillars, or principles, that the church was founded on: 1. Bible-based preaching and teaching; We believe and teach the principles of the Bible. We value preaching the Bible in a simple, practical, yet profound way. 2. Spirit-led living; We value and are obsessed with the person of the Holy Spirit. We totally surrender to His leading. 3. Outreach; We exist to meet the needs of the people in the greater Chicago area and the world! We cherish the opportunity to be a blessing to people. 4. T.O.S.S. (tithing, offering, and seed sowing), We honor the privilege of giving and value giving to God, our church, the less fortunate, and one another.

Simply put, we love to T.O.S.S.! 5. Relevant worship. We seek to create the best worship experience possible. We believe in creating an atmosphere where people can freely express their love and passion for God. 6. Unity: We esteem unity and the vision that God has given our Founder. We do not tolerate, listen, or adhere to statements that cause division. 7. Keeping it real. We believe in speaking the truth in love. We may shock or even surprise you, but in the end, we want to help you grow in Christ. Simply put, we "tell it like it is."

I was excited. I was honored to be asked to sing on the praise team. We did not have a church building, so we worshiped in the auditorium of a local high school.

In 2011, I was starting a new spiritual journey in my

life—inside of a school building. As I eagerly awaited the first service at Faith Movers, thoughts began to roll through my mind. Why would a young pastor leave an established church, existing for more than 30 years, to start a church in a high school? It seemed very risky to me.

Soon after the telephone call with my previous pastor, the praise team was formed, and we began to meet for rehearsals at my former pastor's home. The rehearsals were fun and full of spirit, and I began to establish new relationships. We would often eat at the conclusion of rehearsals and just enjoy each other's company. We sounded good, and that felt good. It was just what I needed.

When it was time for the first service at FMC, I was asked to be there early. The praise team went into the small auditorium of the school and we began to rehearse. Vocally and spiritually, we were in sync, but I still had questions about why we were here and what was going to happen. We completed rehearsal and ended with prayer, and what came next was the time we all waited for.

My new pastor had considered holding service in the small auditorium, which held about 175 to 200 people. We dodged a bullet there because the number of people I saw upon entering the large auditorium far exceeded those numbers. The spirit was high, and I could feel the presence of God—but the jury was still out.

After praise and worship, it was time for the Message. As the pastor began to speak, I was very attentive and focused. It felt like Jesus Himself had put His hand on my shoulder and said, "Just Listen."

As I listened, I was not only hearing the pastor, but I also began to hear from God. I just kept hearing, "Be still and know that I am God." The more I heard that in my spirit, the more I began to realize God had enrolled me in a course on faith that I did not register for.

Or did I?

You see, I had clearly demonstrated challenges in my

waiting season, and despite being in a new season of my life, I still experienced doubt, concern, and fear. I still showed dysfunction in the area of building faith, continuing to move forth without paying attention to what was going on within me. Instead, I was more concerned about the decisions other people were making. So, when I asked for this collaboration of pastors, that was my registration.

When you pay attention to what God is doing in your life, it always feels better. His thoughts are not our thoughts; our ways are not His ways. So, as I continued to sit there and listen, I learned what "be still" truly meant. When developing your faith, being still is not just a position of physical stagnation; it is a calling from God to open your mind and spirit to Him. He does not want you to be focused on your job, that man or woman, or anything else. In developing your faith, you must remove all the irrelevant noise and make the main thing the main thing: God!

I then began quieting my mind and tuned in to the pastor and my Holy Spirit. As I listened, the pastor began sharing aspects of how FMC came to be—basically answering the questions I had in my head. He talked extensively about his faith, the support of his wife, and where the decision came from, and I was completely taken aback. Not only did I not expect him to answer the questions I kept in my head, but he also made me ask myself, "Who has that level of faith?"

I felt that I understood faith, but I was surprised to see that level of faith in action. In his message, my pastor explained how God gave him a command for a new ministry that would be Christ-Centered, Spirit-Led, and Kingdom-Focused. He stated that God began to deal with him internally about beginning this ministry that would focus on reaching lost people. God's desire for him was to lead a church where the Spirit could flow freely, and the outside community could be impacted. He told us how he and his wife decided to walk away from a comfortable lifestyle and step into the unknown. I appreciated the message and his transparency, and I enjoyed singing with the praise team. The overall service was great, the substance was there, but where was the evidence? I registered for this class in faith, and God was faithful in providing it. I would learn that we must trust God to give us what is best, not what we ask for. He has plans for us to prosper...and give hope to our future. Today, I can see how all things were working together for my good, but back then, I still needed evidence.

As we were coming to the end of the service, the pastor extended an invitation to join the church and the family of Christ. I remember walking into the auditorium and seeing a throng of people, but I still had doubts about people joining. I just assumed they did a good job of getting the word out, and it didn't hurt that we were in a high school founded in 1900, so everyone knew where it was. I wondered who would want to be a part of a church that congregated in a school, and at that moment, it was as if God said, "You want evidence? Here it is."

Approximately 500 people went up to the front of the auditorium to accept Christ and to become part of FMC. I had never witnessed anything like it before. I walked out of that auditorium overjoyed and with a lot to digest. I clearly knew that God was working on me, preparing me for something, but I had no clue what it was. All I knew was that I could look in one direction and see my previous pastor, who poured a great deal into me; having him there gave me a sense that I was in the right place. In the other direction, I could see this young pastor, who had just given me a lesson in faith that affected me in a great way that I will never forget.

I did not know how long this class in faith was going to last or how long I would be a student, but I left that first service feeling more comfortable and at ease. It wasn't anything that I did—it was all God. All I had to do was "be still and know." Looking back, it should have been simple, but I was still working on my ability to wait. The "be still and know" step was yet another challenge—one that I felt I wanted to face and conquer.

In case you are wondering, on the morning of June 12th, 2011, I was one of the approximately 500 that joined FMC. Today, I realize that although I joined FMC, I wouldn't become a Faith Mover until several years later.

Despite having just seen it demonstrated, I felt like achieving that level of faith was close to impossible. As much as I wanted to question and dispute it, I could not; my eyes and ears were just witnesses to what faith can produce. I grew up in a culture that said things like, "A bird in the hand is worth two in the bush." My pastor pursued the "two in the bush." Why give up something that you have and risk losing it to go after something that isn't guaranteed? I got my answer the morning of that first service: unwavering faith. What makes sense to one person may be nonsensical to another. When I think about it, the way culture has influenced our thinking and beliefs, no wonder unwavering faith is such a difficult thing to achieve. In Matthew 19:26, Jesus said while discussing with His disciples the gift of salvation, "With men, this is impossible; but with God, all things are possible." I knew I had to build my relationship with God, but what did that look like? "All things are possible" was a pretty big statement, in my opinion. But evidence began popping up all around me.

As time went by, the church grew exponentially. Our outreach programs were such a success. We were giving and providing for those in need. I could see the operation of the 7 pillars—but the biggest piece of evidence I saw was unbelievable. Within two years of the ministry's beginning, we were able to purchase our own church! I believe that if things happen and you just cannot explain it, you can be sure it was God. Having recently bought a home, I understood what it took to purchase property. And the church's new property exceeded 60,000 square feet, including a sanctuary, gymnasium, school, and much more. Being that we were a relatively young, nonprofit ministry, I knew that getting a loan to purchase a building with that much square footage would be next to impossible, but FMC was on the move.

"Be still and know that I am God" grew clearer to me. We must know Him and what He wants from us. Ephesians 4:15 says, "Instead, we will speak the truth in love, growing in every way more and more like Christ, who is the head of his body, the church." Becoming more and more like Christ meant that I had to know Him on a much deeper level than I did at that time. Knowing Him meant spending time with Him, discovering myself, and developing the ability to hear His voice. This seemed like a tall task for me, but I was ready. I had seen extreme faith at work, and I saw what it produced. I saw the substance and, finally, the evidence. Joining FMC was a Godsend. I really felt myself growing in faith and in the knowledge of God. God had answered my prayers and He gave me the opportunity to witness everything that I had questioned, and I could feel my faith getting stronger and stronger. I felt that my class had to be coming to an end, and I was ready to begin preparations for my graduation.

Jeremiah 29:11 says, "'For I know the plans I have for you,' declares the Lord, 'plans to prosper you and not to harm you, plans to give you hope and a future.'" I decided I had it all figured out and I was ready to move on; it was as if I knew God's plan for me and I had achieved it. Little did I know, I had yet to fully carry the plan out. When God speaks to you and shows you signs and wonders, buckle up and enjoy the ride. He does not think, or act like us. We must be careful not to take the baton from Him and run our final leg of the race. I thought I was close to graduation, but I had not even finished the course. Going ahead of God is dangerous, which is why we must place the word of God in our hearts and protect it. I thought the wait, the being still and knowing God, was tough—not in the least bit. There was more in store for me. The journey God has set out for you is filled with surprises—surprises that can rock your very core. Storm clouds rose in my life, but things got better—or so I thought.

Chapter Four

"Stand firm then, with the belt of truth buckled around your waist, with the breastplate of righteousness in place, and with your feet fitted with the readiness that comes from the gospel of peace. In addition to all this, take up the shield of faith, with which you can extinguish all the flaming arrows of the evil one. Take the helmet of salvation and the sword of the spirit, which is in the word of God."
– Ephesians 6:14-17

It was late 2013, and things were looking up. FMC was doing wonderful things and I felt I was growing. My children had both headed off to college to begin their journey into adulthood. Professionally, I am a Life Skills Trainer, Life Coach, and Public Speaker. My business was doing fine; however, I was experiencing health issues.

For much of my adult life, I battled with arthritis—more specifically, gout. I have several family members that have experienced the same condition. The symptoms of gout are fever, sudden severe pain, and swelling in one or more joints. The pain was excruciating. Gout can be triggered by several foods: red meats, organ meats, and seafood-rich purine, to name a few. In addition, sweetened drinks and, of course, alcohol. Unfortunately, I enjoyed a drink every now and then—more now than then. It was a key part of the social construct I held with my crew, and I felt my culture might be disappointed if I let that go. So, I faced a quandary.

Pain is an amazing thing; it can get your attention when nothing else can. It led me to research and find out as much as I could about this medical condition. I began to take steps to manage my gout when an attack came, but when the pain subsided, I went back to living as irresponsibly as I was before the pain hit. I am reminded of the adage, "When you know better, you do better." I guess for me, I needed a definition of "better."

I did what I felt was necessary to manage the pain. I gave in to the belief that if it does not hurt, there's no need to do anything about it. I could have done more, but after researching and feeling a little bit better, the need subsided, and I pressed on. My gout never got better. As a matter of fact, it got even worse, and I was responsible for not managing my gout correctly. Although I felt like I was ready to graduate this class in faith, based on everything I saw going on around me, I still was neglecting all that was going on within me. My armor was lacking. I had no breastplate, my belt and shield were missing, and my sword was noticeably short. Without most of what I needed to fight off the attacks of the enemy, I was very vulnerable. Although I was faithful in attending church, I was not faithful in attending to myself. I was not being my genuine self. As much as I saw what God was doing in my life, I did not know that, within a season of transition, there will be things you must release in order to receive what God has for you. Because there were people and things that I had not released yet, I was not positioned to fully receive. So, if armor is meant to guard you against the attacks of the enemy, I stood naked—a prime target.

The waiting season can be long and arduous, especially when you are not operating in genuine authenticity. I found that the recipe for waiting is one that can be somewhat elusive. I believed that I was on the right track before realizing that I was not. There were a few things I needed to recognize during my waiting season: who I was waiting for, where the weight was coming from, and how to exhibit confidence in my prayer request. I understand that the season of wait can be challenging, but I never met the challenge. I believed that I was doing all that I needed to do and that everything would be fine. I didn't think that I was missing the mark, but I was. I may not have been as faith-filled as I wanted to be, but I felt I was not that far off. The reality is, I was worse off than I thought.

This was just the start of my journey to unwavering faith, and I had much more ahead of me. I only wish I knew exactly what was coming.

I continued to have gout attacks, some more severe than others. Being an independent contractor, I had some flexibility in my schedule—helpful for when my gout would attack my body. During these attacks, my wife and children were very instrumental in my care. Although I was stubborn, proud, and pigheaded, they stuck by me and cared for me. I did not make it easy for them, but their awesome love and concern for me were truly their motivation.

One day, I had a training scheduled in Springfield, Illinois (about two hundred miles away) and I was going to drive there, provide the training, and drive back. A few days before I was to leave, the gout came. As always, I was determined to go because I refused to allow this thing to keep me from doing what I loved and what brought money into my household. On the morning I was to leave, I was in the midst of a severe attack. It was so severe that I was not able to get out of my recliner for the two days leading up to my trip. When I got up, with my wife's assistance, I proceeded to my car to leave. I got all the way to my car, but I was unable to get in. The pain was in my feet as well as my knees, and I was completely unable to drive. Feeling defeated, I returned to my basement and my recliner. I felt less than a man. Dejected and miserable, I wondered how I could allow this thing to control me to such a degree. What was I going to do? For the next few months, I continued along, business as usual. Then, sometime after that gout attack, another health issue appeared.

CHAPTER FIVE

*"The Lord said to Satan,
'Very well, then, he is in your hands,
but you must spare his life.'"*
– Job 2:6

I had my first of three seizures. There was no history of seizures in my family, so this condition came out of nowhere. These experiences were both frightening and life changing.

When the first seizure occurred, I was away from home visiting friends. They were able to call an ambulance and get me to the hospital. I was unconscious and when I finally regained consciousness, there were so many people that had come to visit me, and I felt so much love but seeing the faces of my wife and children really shook me up. I looked mortality in the face for the very first time. In my moment of fear, I began to pray. I asked God to save my life and to please tell me what to do. I was lost with no answers. To be unconscious and helpless for I don't know how long, anything could have happened to me. I was not in control. All I knew was to pray.

As I was praying for my life to be saved, I called on the name of the Lord, but I did not hear from Him. I heard from the medical staff as they informed me of my condition, telling me how severe my blood pressure was, how much medication I needed, and how dire things were. I began another season of wait. I waited for results. I waited for medications. I waited for the manifestation of the medications. Waiting, I began to feel frustrated and unsure of my future. A few days later, I was back in my home, surrounded by my loved ones, and I began to relax, feel more content, and to focus on God.

In that moment of calm, stillness, and reverencing God, He allowed me to revisit all that happened to me while

I was in the hospital: experiencing the seizure, the people that were there to help me, regaining consciousness in the hospital, feeling so much love and concern from family and friends, dipping into a state of fear and frustration, receiving information about my medical condition, and finally being released to my loved ones.

I realized He was there all along. He got me to the hospital. He brought me back to consciousness. He brought the loved ones to the hospital. He provided the medical staff with the information they gave me. He restored me so that I could return to my loved ones. He never left me. My mother used to say, "A hard head makes a soft behind." Well, my behind was like cotton! He was showing me that I was not ready to graduate; I still had work to do. He was showing me that He was faithful and just. John 1:9 says, "If we confess our sins, He is faithful and [forgives] us from all unrighteousness." God was showing me substance as well as evidence! I felt that I finally understood. But in reality, I still had more to experience and more to learn. Word to the wise: Do not try to graduate early. He knows the plans He has for your life; you do not.

So, the attacks did not stop. I thought I was about to get my cap and gown, but I still had not finished the class. I continued going to church, I got my medication, and I followed the prescribed game plan for my health. I was doing all the right things, so I thought.

When I experienced my second seizure, I was working, providing training to help the staff to stay connected and viable as a team. Things were going well, and it came time to take a break. I left the training and went upstairs to use the restroom. The next thing I knew, I was in a hospital being told that I had a seizure. The last thing I remember was being alone in the restroom. A colleague of mine later told me that he found me there on the floor.

I could have died that day, but I was not alone. God was there. God saved me. "God is our refuge and strength, always ready to help in times of trouble" (Psalm 46:1).

This experience affected me differently. The first time, people were there; this time I was all alone. God was showing me that He was true to His word. So, I began talking to God: When was I going to fully trust and depend on Him? I was frustrated with myself. I am not a stupid man, so why was I not getting this? I had experienced several seasons of wait. I had my prayers answered. I was in a church that was filling me with the word of God and showing me example after example of what real faith looks like and the results it could bring, so why was this taking me so long? When God is preparing you for something, have an open mind; the only way you can prepare yourself is to be unequivocally submitted to Him. I wasn't quite there yet.

When I experienced my third seizure, I was, again, on a job. However, the previous job was with a company I had been with for more than 20 years. This job was with a new company, within Chicago proper. I was accustomed to working in the South Suburbs, closer to home. Arriving at the facility, I was pumped, feeling on top of my game. It was my first day working there, and I was hoping to develop a long-standing relationship with them.

I delivered the training to completion, and I felt good about the prospect of an ongoing relationship. When the woman that hired me chose to walk me to my car, I really felt that I had done a great job. Being accompanied to my car by a client was not usual for me, so I saw this as a good sign.

On the way, we talked about how well the training went and how things would look moving forward. I was about to get in my car and leave, but the next thing I knew, I was in a hospital—not a hospital in the South Suburbs where I lived, but one in Chicago. I had experienced my third seizure and, this time, I was with a group of complete strangers—all except one person who seemed to be there every time I had that experience: God!

This one was extra scary because had it come seconds later, I would have been behind the wheel of my car driving home. I thought about the woman who had walked me to my car. I felt sorry that she had to see and experience that, but I was glad God placed her there. I was full of joy and fear at the same time. While in the hospital, I had visitors, but there were not as many as my two previous hospital stays.. My family came to visit, but many of the people who didn't, lived further away. When you are scared and in trouble, you would like to think that every one that came to see you the first time would surely come to see you now, but that was not the case. Yeah, I had visitors, but my mind started playing tricks on me. I began to wonder, why were people not coming to visit, was the hospital too far, or had they given up on me? Did they think that this was some form of me crying wolf, or was it that they never really loved me? This was clearly the worst of my hospital stays, but it was also the most important one of my life.

Even through all those negative thoughts, God was there. He secured that contract. He gave me the strength to make it through the training. He sent that woman to walk me to my car, and He prevented me from getting in that car. Once again, I was focused on what was happening outside of me without giving any substantive attention to all that needed to be fixed within me. We can get so consumed with the majesty of God, how He shows His constant presence in our lives, that we neglect to do what we need to do in order to position ourselves to receive all that He has for us. I am reminded of a familiar scripture that I have read and known for many years: "The thief comes only to steal, kill, and destroy you, but I have come that you may have life, and life more abundantly" (John 10:10).

When you forget about him—wait, who? I'm talking about the enemy: the prince of darkness, Beelzebub, Lucifer, the tempter, Satan—the devil. If he is forgotten, you might find yourself questioning your church, questioning your pastor, questioning your loved ones, or even questioning God. The enemy is always on the job, particularly when you show signs of growing closer to God. Don't ever be confused; Jesus told us plainly what the enemy is here to do. John 10:10 is clear. Jeremiah 29:11 is clear. God is our friend. He wants to help us, never harm us. Allowing yourself to doubt that and absorb thoughts and emotions that are not of God exposes your weaknesses. Like any lying, conniving, and deceitful being, the enemy will take advantage of that and attack you even harder. Do not allow your doubts or confusion to encourage Satan's tricks and deceit. God is the way, the truth, and the light. Isaiah 26:3 says, "You will keep Him in perfect peace whose mind is stayed on you because He trusts in you." Therefore, it is so important for us to have on the full armor of God. The helmet of salvation and the sword of the spirit are vital. The helmet protects our command center, the brain. When our command center is unprotected and gets damaged, the rest of the armor is greatly affected. We must put on the helmet and secure it firmly so that messages of doubt and fear, or any opinion raised against the majesty and true existence of God, are deflected. Once the helmet is secure, the sword of the spirit becomes our fuel to keep us moving forward in the direction of unwavering faith.

My stay in the hospital was a moment that I did not ask for, but I understood why it was necessary. Once again, God restored me, and I was able to return home to my loved ones. This time, I was more appropriately prepared; I had my helmet, my sword, and my gospel of peace. I was being fitted for my breastplate, but my belt was still on layaway.

Now you would think that, after dealing with several seizures, ongoing gout attacks and excessive hypertension (my numbers were in the 200s/100s), I would have put on the full armor of God. That was not the case. I continued attending church, receiving a fresh word, but I also stepped up my B.I.B.L.E. game: Basic Instructions Before Leaving Earth, an appropriate phrase for my current state of being. I was reading the Bible with a different focus and intensity. I wanted to learn. I wanted to apply it to my life.

Still on the path toward being my authentic self, I admit I was concerned that, since it took me so long to get to this point in my journey, maybe I was too late. I spent time sending encouraging messages to people on social media, and that's when and where I did most of my Bible research. While I think it is a great use of one's time—it's important to pour into and encourage others, and it is what I love to do—why didn't I apply some of that Bible research to my own life?

When you make your request known to God, brace yourself. I had prayed to God about my direction and defining my authentic self, and I really felt that I was evolving in my knowledge and understanding of God. One day, as I was researching scripture to bless the people of God, I stumbled upon this: "The Lord is not slow in keeping His promise, as some understand slowness. Instead, He is patient with you, not wanting anyone to perish, but everyone to come to repentance" (Peter 3:9). After digesting that, I knew that I was not too late; God was patient with me. Because I was missing pieces of my armor, I did not yet see God's patience. God was still waiting for me, and although I wanted to be closer to Him, to know Him better, I needed to make a transition.

Entering into a season of transition is different from entering into a season of wait. The world, or your culture, has a hold on you that is hard to break away from. You have been a part of it for most if not all your life. Remember, in the first chapter, I wrote about not wanting to disappoint my culture? Well, disappointment is going to happen as you transition. There will be some things that you do not understand and some things that you do not want to transition from. To get what God has in store for you, you must let go of some things: people, places, and ways of thinking. It is a season when you must F.R.O.G. (Fully Rely on God).

That is why I joined FMC. That is why I had health issues. I needed to learn how to F.R.O.G. "Do not conform to the patterns of this world but be transformed by the renewing of your mind. Then you will be able to test and approve what

God's will is—his good and perfect will. Then you will learn to know God's will for you, which is good and pleasing and perfect" (Romans 12:2). I wanted good. I wanted pleasing. I wanted perfect. I wanted everything God had for me. But I didn't feel comfortable leaving and disappointing my culture. So much was going to have to change—I was going to have to change. Who would be in my new crew and what would we do? I had been loyal to my culture all my life, and now I was questioning it. Having one foot in the world and the other in the gospel can be very stressful, and it was beginning to weigh on me. I knew I had a choice to make. After much thought and plenty of prayer, I decided to enter my season of true transition.

Chapter Six

"I, the Lord thy God, will hold thy right hand, saying unto thee, fear not; I will help thee."
– Isaiah 41:13

In 2014, I was still on my journey toward unwavering faith, and my mission was to fight against conforming to the ways of the world. We are to be in the world but not of the world. The world offers things that we know are wrong, but we accept them anyway. To resist conforming to the ways of the world was no small undertaking; it meant that I had to judge what others did.

Wait! I was looking outside of myself again. I knew it would take looking inward and judging myself.

I had been conforming in many ways to my culture and releasing that, would be difficult. See, once you conform, your culture has a difficult time accepting your transition. They like the way you were, and they would always know you as that person. This is why you must be "steadfast and unmovable, always abounding in the work of the Lord." (1Corinthians 15:58). Consistency and genuineness matter. You will have your naysayers and your "looks like a duck, quacks like a duck" prognosticators who will never be comfortable with you as you walk into your destiny.

I forged ahead, determined to do what felt right for me. Although I felt confident in my goal, I knew that I needed the Lord to hold my hand along the journey. I understood that He would be there and, though He may not guide me, He would help me. As I focused on areas in my life where I fell short, I felt a shift in me that I had never felt before. This was not just about me, but this was also about the people I was intricately connected to—primarily, those I lived with. This journey was more than I anticipated.

I had been married for fourteen years, and I was causing damage in this relationship. I was as neglectful to that aspect of my life as I was to my individual life. I was not as loving, nurturing, or attentive as I should have been as a husband. Had I been more transparent and honest with myself, maybe I would have been. "Do not be deceived: God cannot be mocked. A man reaps what he sows" (Galatians 6:7).

Disagreements and arguments began to happen more often, and my marriage headed toward dissolution. I felt that all hope was lost, and I did not want counseling. As I continued on my journey—being enriched by my church as well as reading, understanding, and preserving the word in my heart—I remained hopeful. Though I felt I was moving toward adorning my breastplate of righteousness, I was still using thoughts and behaviors that would ultimately end my marriage. I thought that my experience of working with people and couples over the years would come in handy; all I needed to do was utilize my learned skills in order to turn things around. Proverbs 3:5 says, "Trust in the Lord with all your heart and lean not on your own understanding." I was trusting my heart, believing that I would be able to talk this thing through and have it all worked out. I took the baton from God. Did I trust the Lord? Yes, but I thought this was a situation I could handle on my own. Well, as it turned out, I couldn't. I let go of God's hands and I traveled this road alone. We argued, we talked—we talked, we argued. Nothing was helping. My marriage ended in 2016.

The end of my marriage was traumatic for me. I thought I would be married to this woman for life; that was the way this was supposed to go. I understood I might have to let go of some things during this transition, but I never thought it would be my marriage. Was this God's will for my life, or was this Satan's will? All I knew was that I needed the Lord to hold my hand and help me navigate the unfamiliar, tough terrain. I dropped the ball and I felt bad about it. Of course, I stood strong (never let them see you sweat) and held it together, but all along, I felt the disappointment of not fulfilling my vows—a heavy weight in my spirit. What kind of person was I? I didn't fight for it. I didn't change for it. I was a failure.

As I was contemplating my next move, my wife and I discussed how the separation would look—who would take what, who would keep what. This was really happening! It was like I was watching a bad movie. The reality of things started to sink in, but leading up to the separation, I stood strong. My faith had taken a huge hit, but I was not going to show any signs of weakness. Because I made the decision to do things my way, we were now looking at dissolution.

Part of the separation process was figuring out where I was going to live. Everything moved so fast, or maybe I was in denial. Either way, I was not prepared to leave. One day, I was home while my wife was at work, and I received a telephone call. The woman on the line told me about an available room in her home and that I was welcome to live there. I responded, "Yes, and thank you!" This was a godsend, and I would soon find out just how big of a godsend it was. God was still there, holding my hand every step of the way. I felt a great relief: Now everything would be OK. I would live there for a few months and then I would find my own place—sounded like a good plan to me.

It was especially important that I focus on myself in order to heal and correct things that needed correcting. Do not, for one second, forget who the ultimate tactician is, the one who has a plan for your life, the one who has a plan that is different than yours: The Head of your life is God! When I did not have a place to go, God sent an "angel" to help me. He told me He was there to help me, and He did. I grew stronger in my faith.

This "angel" is a person I have known all my life, but I know her invitation was orchestrated by God. It was my sister—the same sister that introduced me to the church she so enjoyed. My sister, who happened to be married to my former pastor. Sometimes, God will bring you full circle in order to reinforce all that you need to move forward. I not only had my FMC pastor, but I also had my brother-in-law and former pastor pouring into me. God was still answering the prayer that put me at FMC, but I was now with both men on a different level. These two mighty men had come together the way God intended. I didn't know that I would need this reinforcement at the time of my separation, but God knew. Trust God with all your heart and He will help you in times of trouble. Although I was not divorced yet, I did not foresee any trouble. I felt that I could keep my plan in place of reestablishing my independence in a few months. God made sure that I was safe, secure, and in a place where His unyielding love would be demonstrated each and every day. I don't think I could've handpicked a better place.

On March 1st, 2016, I moved into their home. I could now relax and pursue more opportunities to work, all while growing spiritually. I was still dealing with the feeling of disappointment from letting God down by failing to carry out the commitment I made in my vows, but I knew that I had to find a way to put that behind me and continue to work on my health, my career, and my spiritual growth. I was prepared to continue toward unwavering faith. In my heart, I realized that I wanted this level of faith. The price I had to pay to get there would be steep. I knew that I had to fully commit to God, and that was still a problem for me. I was beginning to shed some of the people and places from my life that were not benefiting me on my journey, but I had no idea what was ahead of me.

While I was thinking that the worst was over, the worst—or maybe, in a way, it was the best—was yet to come. I once heard someone say, "Hope for the best, prepare for the worst, and take whatever life throws your way." That quote sounds good but, how do you prepare for the worst when you don't know what the worst could possibly be? I felt I had experienced the worst. What could be worse than letting God down? I had gotten over the hump. I was finally grasping who

I was, and again, I felt I was positioned to really be myself and demonstrate my newfound level of faith in God.

Chapter Seven

"There hath no temptation taken you, but such as is common to man: but God is faithful, who will not suffer you to be tempted above that ye are able; but will with temptation also make a way of escape, that ye may be able to bear it."
— 1Corinthians 10:13

I began to visualize my upcoming move and how that would define yet another chapter in my life. I had been given a reprieve and I was going to take advantage of it; I had the chance to recoup some of what I lost and refocus toward things I wanted to achieve. Even though my marriage ended, I felt victorious¬–though there was still a deficit in my heart for failing the promise "till death do us part." But staying optimistic was the key. I was excited about the opportunities ahead of me: opportunities to develop new professional contracts, opportunities to experience independence, to grow toward God, and perform pure self-assessment. With this focus, I would move in the direction of a better life.

I was looking forward to new challenges and new opportunities. Knowing that God was with me, nothing could deter me. "Yea, though I walk through the valley of the shadow of death, I will fear no evil, for Thou art with me; thy rod and thy staff, they comfort me" (Psalm23:4). This scripture reassured me that I was not alone and that He would be there to help me; I would have an escape from any attack or temptation. One of the most popular ways to escape temptation is to turn it into behavior. This is not the way of escape that Paul was speaking of in 1Corinthians 10:13: "No temptation has overtaken you except what is common to mankind. And God will not let you be tempted beyond what you can bear, and when you are tempted, He will provide a way for you to endure it." However, it is an escape. Fortunately, I was given an escape that was tailored for me: I was living with my sister and my former pastor, and my new life was beginning. God placed me in a direction that I was comfortable with and that I clearly understood. All the other issues that I was dealing with, namely my health issues, were far from my mind.

I spoke earlier about two things: the influence of pain and the job description of the enemy. Somehow, at this juncture of my journey, I did not see any evidence of either, and that gave me confidence that I was moving in the right direction. However, it's when you are moving in the right direction that the attack of the enemy becomes fiercest.

My gout and hypertension reminded me that they were still very prevalent in my life. On Thursday, May 5th, 2016, only two months after I moved in, I had a severe gout attack. At urgent care, they took my vitals and told me that my blood pressure was too high and that I needed to be rushed to the hospital. Other than the pain from the gout, I felt fine. I guess I had dealt with hypertension for so long that when my blood pressure was extremely high, I didn't have any symptoms. I was alert and talking while I was in the ambulance—it was the first ambulance trip that I was conscious for. I did not recognize it at the time, but my being conscious would be important during this hospital visit.

We arrived at the hospital and I was immediately admitted. I learned that my kidneys were severely damaged, operating at an extremely low percentage. I was alert, concerned, and focused, so I was able to digest every word they were saying. But as they spoke, my mind drifted to Isaiah 54:17: "No weapon formed against thee shall prosper, and every tongue that shall rise against thee in judgment thou shalt condemn. This is the heritage of the servants of the Lord, and their righteousness is of me, saith the Lord." I began to pray to the Lord the first part of that scripture, repeating "no weapon formed against me shall prosper" over and over again.

As the discussion went on, they began to ask me questions, and those questions gave me a clear picture of how serious this was. I had dealt with hypertension most of my life and I never had any symptoms from it, and I was managing my gout with ibuprofen. The chronic hypertension coupled with the excessive use of ibuprofen had decimated my kidneys. My stomach was in knots, but I was still believing in God's word, believing that this diagnosis would never come to fruition. I had plans—I had more to do. God would never bring me this far to put something like dialysis on my plate. I began to call on the name of Jesus: "You are a healer. You would never put more on me than I can bear, and your word never returns to you void."

After all the recent twists and turns, being without a spiritual covering to the ending of my marriage, I thought the worst was over—but now, I was told I needed dialysis. Once again, I found myself in an unfamiliar area, and all the experience I had gained throughout the years was not going to help. "Trust in the Lord with all thine heart and lean not unto thine own understanding. In all your ways, acknowledge Him, and He will direct your path" (Proverbs 3:5-6). I understood that He knew the plans He had for me and that He would never hurt me, but what I did not understand was—why me? I know that I struggled in my waiting season, and I know that I needed evidence to prove to me the level of faith that had been demonstrated before me, but I couldn't believe those were His reasons for putting me through this. Didn't He realize what this was going to do to me? I had plans I needed to carry out. I didn't want to live in my family's home for long; I was ready to move on and start my new life. I was attending church, singing on the praise team, and reading my Bible. My crew was down to a few people, and I worked hard to try and eliminate my ineffective and negative behaviors, so I just didn't understand. Where was I going wrong? I was beginning to feel some frustration as well as some fear.

Chapter Eight

"I have told you all this so that you may have peace in me. Here on earth, you will have many trials and sorrows. But take heart, because I have overcome the world."
– John 16:33

While in the hospital, I was taken into surgery to have a catheter inserted into my stomach. This was necessary for me to be able to receive peritoneal dialysis treatment at home. After being released from the hospital, I was to attend a two-week training at a dialysis center to learn how to administer the treatment myself. Suddenly, I was living a new life, but it was not the life I had hoped or intended to have. At the root of your disappointments are your expectations, and I was swimming in disappointment. I've never felt that low before in my life. My future was so uncertain, but I never gave up on God.

On the morning of my first training, I found out that my sister and my brother-in-law would be attending training with me. This was the reinforcement and support I needed. I could still see God in my life, but I continued to question why God allowed this to happen to me. At the dialysis clinic, I acknowledged that I was with people that I knew loved and cared for me, and after meeting my nurse—who was warm, welcoming, and patient—I felt a calm come over me. I had been reading the Bible with a new purpose and was beginning to hear the voice of God more clearly. There was a scripture that I could remember and relate to my circumstance. I had read the book of Genesis plenty of times, but on that day, I received a different interpretation. "It is not good for the man to be alone; I will make a helper suitable for him" (Genesis 2:18). I know God was speaking of Eve, but that day, God sent me those who fit the significance of "suitable helpers."

We were at the clinic eight hours a day for a couple of weeks; the training was tedious but rewarding. When it was over, my brother-in-law came to me and said, "Don't worry, I got your back." I so needed to hear those words. It was as if he knew what I needed when I needed it. This gave me comfort moving forward, but I still needed direction.

The process of peritoneal dialysis is interesting. The time you are on the machine can be anywhere from two to ten hours, and you do this every day at home. At first, it sounded overwhelming and daunting, but after much prayer, receiving assistance from my brother-in-law, and listening to God, I became more comfortable with it. As I prayed more, I heard from God more, and I focused on listening to His voice. Reflecting on how God orchestrated things in my life from FMC to moving into my former pastor's home, I could hear God saying, "My word never returns to me void." He was helping me just as He said, but He never explained the dialysis.

Where was my way of escape? The question haunted me. I did not feel that such misfortune was necessary, particularly just after leaving my marriage. I thought to myself, "That's it! Perhaps God is punishing me because I disappointed Him by giving up on my marriage." As one of my friends put it, "That was some bad theology!" So, I kept thinking and realized, maybe it wasn't that I disappointed God; maybe I just disappointed myself. Did I even love myself anymore? Hebrews 13:8 says, "Jesus Christ is the same yesterday, today, and forevermore."

He wasn't disappointed in me; I was disappointed in me. I needed to regain self-love. In a critical moment of weakness, I allowed myself to think that God was punishing me. I took my armor off and went against His word. Whenever you go against the word of the Lord, you are asking for trouble. "He will not let your foot slip. He who watches over you, He will not slumber" (Psalms 12:13).

What was I doing? I was so eager for an explanation as to

why I was on dialysis that I fabricated one. Chapter forty of Isaiah talks about knowing that even a young man gets weary, but those that wait on the Lord will be renewed. I didn't wait. I was looking for my way of escape, but in my moment of weakness, I opened the door for Satan. Making room for the enemy was the last thing I wanted to do. If the enemy sees a crack in your armor, the enemy will attack. I wasn't aware that I was making room for the enemy, but when you doubt God and His Word, it doesn't demonstrate faith, and faith was what I was seeking. I had felt like I was moving in the direction of unwavering faith but, with one slip of my mind's tongue, I felt like I was starting over. But I had come so far and given up so much, I did not want to start over.

I was determined to conquer this dialysis and continue worshiping and growing in God. This was not going to set me back. I was going to trust in God with all my heart and would no longer give in to my thoughts or my insecurities. I was not going to fear the enemy. He had come in my health. He came in my marriage. He had been in my life far too long, and it was time for me to take back all that he had taken from me. I was going to be victorious! No devil in hell was going to stop me.

Chapter Nine

*"Be ye angry, and sin not.
Let not the sun go down upon your wrath;
neither give place to the devil."
– Ephesians 4:26*

I gave the enemy a sign that I was about to regress, and he used it as an opportunity to destroy me, but I was not going to allow him to win. I was more determined than ever to get through this—now fully dressed and ready for battle. 2Corinthians 10:3-4 says, "For though we walk in the flesh, we do not war after the flesh. For our weapons of our warfare are not carnal, but mighty through God to the pulling down of strongholds." An act of faith was the only way I was going to beat this thing and turn my life around. I was a professional life skills trainer, and God allowed me to call on the skills of that role. I knew that God was in control, but my choices and decisions were all on me. My words suggested that the enemy had some control over me, but I know that he didn't. I allowed doubt to enter my life, but it was time to kick the enemy out.

I was in control of myself, and I was not about to give him the opportunity to steal my faith, kill my spirit, or destroy my life. All the trials and tribulations that I had endured, I endured them by the grace of God. I reflected on all that I had to deal with over the past five or six years, and it energized me. It gave me hope and direction to face this pivotal time in my life. John 14:26 says, "But I will leave you a comforter, which is the Holy Ghost, whom the Father will send in my name. He shall teach you all things and bring all things to your remembrance, whatsoever I have said unto you." I was now guided by the Holy Spirit, the one that teaches and leads you to recall what you have been taught. He was there all along, but because of my doubts, fears, and overall disobedience, I did not recognize him. I knew that the enemy would not stop. Because I had not given my life completely to God, the enemy sought entry into my life and I had opened the door, but I was determined to keep his influence in my life to a bare minimum.

I often prayed to God to seek direction, asking, "How should I go about handling this dialysis and getting my life back on track?" The only response I heard in my spirit was, "Do the work." I was not quite sure what that meant, but I was not about to give up on God because I didn't understand, so I tried to live my life as normal as I could. I continued to work, attend FMC, and encourage others.

The dialysis was demanding. I would go to the clinic maybe once a week, I would see my nephrologist once a month, and I had periodic appointments with my primary doctor. All the while, my nurse and I grew closer and that gave me comfort and reassured me that God was still in control. She was encouraging and provided me with important information regarding receiving a kidney transplant. I would sometimes have to go to the University of Illinois Hospital, and this is where I signed up to get on the kidney transplant list. To increase my odds, I also went up to the Wisconsin (UW) Health University Hospital and got on the list up there. I decided on these two hospitals because it's best that you are near your hospital in case you have to arrive there in a short amount of time.

One day at home, after taking my treatment, I had chills and a fever. Because my fever was so high, I was taken to the hospital. There was a time I would not have gone to the hospital because of a fever, but I was different now—more obedient. They kept me in the hospital for observation and we eventually learned I had an infection. Infections while on dialysis can be serious. I acquired mine because of a hole, the size of a pin, in my catheter. I had to stay in the hospital for a few days because they needed to put in a new catheter in my upper chest so that I could begin a new type of treatment, hemodialysis, which required going to the dialysis center three times a week for treatment.

The entire incident was nothing but an inconvenience. If this was the best the enemy had to offer, then I thought it was just funny. I had to get a new catheter and now go into the clinic three times a week—is that all you got? I laughed at the enemy. If this is what you call a fierce attack, then I know that it's true: God would not put more on you than you can bear.

As someone who prioritizes freedom, having such a frequent medical commitment was not ideal. I preferred peritoneal treatment because of the freedom it afforded me yet, I was able to adjust to in-clinic hemodialysis treatment. The hemodialysis treatment required me to be at the clinic by 6:00am three days a week. I was now on a schedule. Peritoneal treatment I could take anytime of the day.

Deuteronomy 31:6 says, "Be strong and courageous. Do not be afraid or terrified because of them, for the Lord your God goes with you, He will never leave you nor forsake you." It is amazing how when you truly understand this, you gain an air of confidence and reassurance.

I continued with hemodialysis for several months before I was released to resume my peritoneal treatment. After resuming my peritoneal treatment, I went into the clinic and met with the social worker to discuss the possibility of starting a support group. Because I now had experience with at home as well as in clinic treatment, I felt that I could provide information that would help patients and their support teams in navigating the dialysis experience. I was given the OK and began to facilitate monthly support group meetings. I felt honored to be given this opportunity and I felt my faith continuing to grow. I was developing into the person I wanted and needed to be.

Chapter Ten

"And the Lord said unto Satan,
'Behold, all that he hath is in thy power;
only upon himself put not forth thine hand.
So, Satan went forth from the presence of the Lord."
– Job 9:12

In 2018, my dialysis treatment was going well, and I had an awesome support system. FMC was growing and new friendships and relationships were blossoming. My health issues were being managed with a regimen of different medications, with help from my oldest daughter, who was now married and the mother of two beautiful girls. My two granddaughters, one and two years old, became my inspiration to continue to fight. I could not imagine leaving them; they were the joy of my life. God put everything that I needed in place.

However, I continued to look in my rear-view mirror. I felt Satan was coming. Despite everything, I was standing strong—rooted and unmovable. My support system not only consisted of my family but also my FMC family, friends, and others I didn't even know. God was pulling out all the stops, but I still felt a sense of foreboding.

At that point, I had been in search of a kidney donor for about a year. Once again, I found myself in a waiting season. Because I had failed in a previous season of wait, I decided to apply the principles that I learned and focus on my relationship with the Holy Spirit.

I was on the right path. No, I was not perfect, but my spirit was more in line with understanding and exhibiting faith. I realized not only will you fail to please God without faith, but you are also ultimately sabotaging yourself. The Lord has so much that He wants to give, but you must be in the right position to receive it. Keeping that position is where the hard work lies. I felt I was positioned to receive all He had to give, feeling confident and glad that I had become more familiar with the Word.

I also stayed aware of Satan. This awareness allowed me to identify who my nemesis was; it kept me more alert, and it provided encouragement for me to stay connected to the Word of God. I have heard people say that you shouldn't give the enemy any credit or acknowledgment. I understand that point of view, but I did just the opposite. Proverbs 28:1 says, "The wicked flee when no one pursues, but the righteous are bold as a lion."

In my confidence, I became bold. I began to proudly proclaim, "I am built for this!" Whatever the devil was preparing to do to me, I was built to withstand it. To truly be built for whatever comes, you must recognize and acknowledge the Builder, you must become familiar with the materials that are necessary to build, and you must make sure that all materials—the armor—are in place and tightly secured. Because I had met these requirements, I was confident my armor would get me through this season of my life, but I knew I could not underestimate Satan. He is always on his job, and he was not going to stop.

During one of my many visits to the doctor, they requested that I have a colonoscopy. After the procedure, they told me they noticed that my prostate was somewhat swollen, and they wanted to perform a biopsy. I continued in my compliance to the medical staff and agreed to schedule the test.

In this particular season of my journey, I began to experience restless leg syndrome. The irresistible urge to move my legs typically happened when my body was at rest. I was focusing on all the things that were going on, and I knew who was at the root: Satan. When I suggested that God was punishing me for ending my marriage, I had opened the door and he entered. He was ramping up his attack, so he thought. Because I was now firmly rooted in my faith, adorned with the full armor of God, I continued on, declaring, "I see you Satan, and no weapon formed against me shall prosper!" There was nothing that was going to stop me from getting what God had for me. After everything I endured, lost, and given on this journey, there was no way that I was not going to achieve my goal.

I was in position to get a donor. A transplant was in my reach, and I was not going to take my eyes off the prize.

The restless leg became a little more intense, and the medication wasn't working. I began to have sleepless nights. My work was being affected because I was so exhausted during the day, I had a hard time staying awake. Driving became more challenging. Behind the wheel of a car, I almost immediately became exhausted. I became a danger to myself and others. I didn't drive far because I was afraid of falling asleep.

Satan had become more aggressive in his attack, and though I faced new challenges, I still stood strong.

I went for the biopsy, and it was very painful. Days passed, and I received the results:

"You have cancer."

Chapter Eleven

"You heard my plea.
Do not close your ears to my cry for relief.
You came near when I called you,
and you said, 'Do not fear.'"
– Lamentations 3:56-57

The result of my biopsy was three words that I will remember for the rest of my life: "You have cancer."

I was alone when I got the news. As the doctor began to talk to me about my options, I began to pray. Devastated, I felt that all hope was lost. I needed God to save me. I had taken every blow from the devil that I could, but this—I did not know how to deal with this.

It was a long walk to my car. By the time I got there, my fear evaporated, and I began to think about how I was going to tell my loved ones. I was no longer worried about myself, but I found myself struggling with having to share the news.

I was greatly shaken by those three words: "You have cancer." I did not question God, but I began to think about the story of Job—all that he endured and lost and how God allowed Satan to test him but not to lay a hand on him. Incredibly, that story inspired me and settled my spirit. I shifted my focus to the words of Job 7:11-12 (NIV), which read, "Therefore, I will not keep silent. I will speak out in the anguish of my spirit; I will complain in the bitterness of my soul." I got in my car and began speaking my new creed. "I was built for this!" I was angry at what the enemy was trying to do to me. "I was built for this." I was not going to allow fear to overtake me. "I was built for this!" The more I said it, the stronger and more confident I became.

My younger sister took the liberty of having sweatshirts

and hoodies printed with my creed on them. They also included a photo of Jesus carrying and bearing the cross. The scripture that accompanied the creed and the photo is Exodus 15:2: "The Lord is my strength and my song; He has given me victory. This is my God, and I will praise Him, my father's God, and I will exalt Him."

I got home and put one of my sweatshirts on before addressing my family. It was my way of reminding myself, the enemy, and anyone that saw me that no demonic force was going to stop me from getting all that God had for me. You can try me, you can test me, but you will soon realize—I am built for this!

I informed my family of the diagnosis and shared all that the doctors told me. It was prostate cancer, and my options were chemotherapy, prostate removal (which would be my last option), and radiation. I did not want to experience the horror stories I had heard about chemotherapy, so I considered radiation and the pros and cons as explained by my doctors. After praying and discussing options with my family, I decided to go with radiation. It was painless and only required several weeks of treatment. I was diagnosed with prostate cancer on January 11th, 2019, and I began my radiation treatment on April 17th.

I continued with my life—providing life skills training to adults, coaching basketball at a Christian school, and facilitating the dialysis support group. I felt that my condition was something I needed to be careful about sharing, so I didn't tell many people. I was determined not to lose this battle. My command from the Lord was to do the work.

Radiation treatment allowed me time to think and be still. Once the session started, I would get situated in the small, tube-like space and immediately close my eyes. I ended up looking forward to these moments when I could relax and spend quiet time with God. Because my restless leg was getting more and more intense, I would be so exhausted during the day; the treatments gave me the opportunity to fall asleep.

My faith and my confidence became second nature to me. I didn't speak much about it; I just walked in the spirit of Hebrews 11:1: "Now, faith is the substance of things hoped for and the evidence of things not seen." I no longer had to see it because I was sure that my prayers would be answered. I would receive a kidney. I had a posture of Psalm 46:10, "Be still and know that I am God." I was not moved by anything other than the presence of God. No attack by the enemy could sway me. God was in control, and I know exactly who He is. No longer was there any question or any doubt as to who God was. I had a John 8:24 mentality: "Unless you believe that I am who I claim to be, you will die in your sins." It wasn't just that I was not prepared to die—I was proclaiming victory over the enemy. God heard my plea, and He was there with me.

One day, I received a telephone call. I braced myself when I saw it was from the University of Illinois Hospital. Maybe this was the call I had been waiting for! Maybe it was news regarding my transplant. I knew God was there and I knew that He would answer my prayer. I answered the phone, and the only words I remember were, "Because of your recent diagnosis of prostate cancer, we must remove you from the transplant list."

Chapter Twelve

*"But when you pray, go into your room,
close your door, and pray to your father, who is unseen.
Then your father, who sees what is done in secret,
will reward you."*
– Matthew 6:6

I had family and friends who were in the process of being evaluated as a donor and others who were already determined not to be a match. But it no longer mattered. This new disease knocked me out of the running to receive transplant surgery, and I was up against the clock. The older you get, the less likely your chances are to receive a transplant. I was 57 years old.

"You intended to harm me, but God intended it for good to accomplish what is now being done: the saving of many lives" (Genesis 50:20). The enemy was outsmarted once again—or was I outsmarted? I felt comfortable where I received my radiation treatment but combating the restless leg syndrome left me exhausted and I would fall asleep while talking to God. The enemy is tricky and conniving, and I did not realize that he was blocking my prayer time. I was not on the transplant list anymore, neither in Chicago nor Wisconsin. What was going on?

I began to reflect on how things were going in my life: a series of seizures, chronic hypertension, divorce, end-stage kidney failure, restless leg syndrome, prostate cancer, and now, removal from the kidney transplant list. All of this in a matter of a few years—I really could not believe it. Some people would have just thrown in the towel and given up, but I knew: "I am built for this!" I continued to hold onto my belief that God would turn it all around. So, I took my mind off the transplant and just focused on my radiation treatment.

It is always an issue for me to tell someone bad news. You do not know how it's going to affect them. You hope that their faith closely resembles yours, but you just don't know. When I told my immediate family, I was no longer on the list, they were encouraging and stood with me in faith. I so appreciated that. I knew that I could not tell everyone, because not everyone would respond with the same level of encouragement and support. I wanted to be wise in the area of sharing. I wanted to stick with God. I had to. Philippians 4:6 states, "Do not be anxious about anything but in every situation, by prayer and petition, with thanksgiving, present your request to God."

God had been so good to me. Now was not the time to turn my back on Him and give in to the attacks.

I had to get rid of this cancer—that was all that I could do. I dug in my heels, never flinched, and I never showed signs of weakness and doubt. Matthew 17:20 says, "Truly, I tell you, if you have faith like a grain of a mustard seed, you can say to this mountain, 'Move from here to there,' and it will move. Nothing will be impossible for you." I love this scripture and I leaned on it all the way through my journey. I was confident that I could move my mountain—the cancer. After my radiation treatment was complete, I went into another season of wait as I waited for the results.

When my treatment ended, the Holy Spirit reminded me of the many blessings I had experienced in the last few years. I increased my faith by believing, praying, and studying. I fought through those seizures and won. I let go of things to put myself in a better position to receive from God. Two mighty men of God came together to facilitate the start of a ministry that I became a part of. I was allowed to witness the work of God in that ministry. I was blessed with a support system that could only have been designed by God. Most of all, I was still here! After reflecting on my victories, my challenges and losses seemed minuscule. I knew that this waiting season was going to be okay, and I would, in the end, achieve victory over cancer and get back on the transplant list.

I left the hospital that day knowing that I was healed of cancer and knowing that God would grant me what I desired: a new kidney. I arrived home in a good mood, believing that all was well.

Although I continued to be challenged with restless leg syndrome, my resolve was stronger. I was more confident than ever that it was just a matter of time before I would have victory over restless leg. This condition became the focus of my attention, primarily because of the effect it had on my life. It had gotten to the point that I was getting one or two hours of not-so-restful sleep. I did not want anyone to know just how exhausted I was, but whenever I was home with my family in a common area of the house, I would fall asleep, and my legs would move as if I had Parkinson's. I had to conquer this somehow, and I was determined to.

Chapter Thirteen

*"Heal me Lord, I will be healed; save me
and I will be saved, for you are the one I praise."*
– Jeremiah 17:14

While the doctors at my dialysis clinic were extremely encouraging, they would remind me of my lab results and that I needed to take better care of myself. My blood tests showed secondary anemia, hypertension, low hemoglobin, high phosphorous, and some fluid retention. Things were not looking good, but faith is the substance of things hoped for, and I was going to continue to hold out hope. Faith is the evidence of things not seen, and though I had not seen God give me a kidney, I knew, in my spirit, that He would.

This tremendous growth in my faith led me to look at my medical conditions in a whole new light. Every seizure I had served to improve my understanding of the importance of health management. My health issues encouraged me to examine myself and take ownership of the part I played in them manifesting.

Although I regretted the dissolution of my marriage, the amount of care and support I needed through this time was not something I would have wanted for my wife and marriage. I know she would have been there and cared for me, but I couldn't imagine putting her through all that was going on with me. The connections I had established on this journey—from my current pastor to FMC, to my current dwelling—were all extremely instrumental in this season and I greatly appreciated all that they provided for me.

I was finding peace and joy while reflecting on my journey. I had begun to accept and understand different aspects of my experience and putting things in perspective was healing and therapeutic for me. I needed that in my life. Thank God for the Holy Spirit operating as Jesus said he would.

In the midst of all that, the enemy continued to try. I was still standing—not only standing but also getting stronger. In the past, there were times I expected things of God and I was disappointed when I did not get them. To minimize those disappointments, I learned to manage my expectations. He did say His ways are not our ways. I stopped attaching dates and times to when I wanted God to move and I remembered Habakkuk 2:3: "For still, the vision awaits its appointed time, it hastens to the end—it will not lie. If it seems slow, wait for it. It will surely come; it will not delay." The Holy Spirit reminded me, "Be anxious for nothing," and that was what I was going to do. I moved with a spirit of calm not because I was faking it, but because I honestly believed that God was going to turn things around. I needed Him to.

Chapter Fourteen

*"Do not mistake God's patience for His absence.
His timing is perfect, and his presence is constant.
He is always with you."*
– Deuteronomy 31:6

On April 26th, 2019, I returned to the hospital to get the results of my radiation treatment. My oldest daughter, the manager of my medication, accompanied me.

The doctor informed us that the treatment was a success. I was now cancer-free!

God did it again. I made sure that I was intentional in my daily prayer. I wanted to make sure that God could see me and my heart. I was desperate for that news. All I could do is give God all the praise for saving my life once again—for bringing me out of darkness into the marvelous light. He is so awesome!

I had cancer and God removed it. He is a promise-keeping God. I knew it and I would forever proclaim it. As I exited the room with my daughter, I rang the bell—a tradition for patients who complete treatment. This signaled victory over whatever was ailing you. I could not wait to get back on the transplant list.

I called the transplant team to tell them of my victory. They informed me that they would speak to the attending physician to confirm my results before discussing what the next steps would be. So, I waited. I was becoming all too familiar with the wait. Waiting on God is one thing; waiting on man is another. I knew that time was of the essence, and the sooner I could be back on the list, the better.

There were many nights when I would cry just to know that there were people in my life who would give me a kidney. Even as I acknowledged those who prayed for me, thought about me, and helped me, Satan still fought against me. He constantly wanted me to judge my family and friends and focus on how few people stepped up, but I continued to be encouraged by Romans 8:1-2: "Therefore, there is now no condemnation for those who are in Christ Jesus, because the law of the spirit has set you free from the law of sin and death."

I rebuked the enemy every time any thought that was not of God would enter my spirit. I was well-loved by many, and I returned that love. Everyone who was in my life was assigned to give me what they could. Whether it was thoughts, prayers, a phone call, a visit—I want them all to know that I greatly appreciated and needed their offering, and I did not take it for granted. I would list all the names of those who shared their offering with me, but that would take up too many pages in this publication. My love for them is strong. Take that, Satan!

I knew that I needed to remain faithful and diligent. My lab numbers were still a challenge, my blood pressure was not being effectively managed, and this restless leg was still affecting me. While it was not painful at all, it had to be the most annoying condition that I was dealing with. Through it all, I just needed to stay committed in my prayer life.

I know that God is a healer and that His word never returns to Him void. The Gospel acted as my armor, and it wouldn't have been available to me if I hadn't known the Word of God. 1Samuel 17:38-39 says, "Then Saul dressed David in his tunic. He put a coat of armor on him and a bronze helmet on his head. David fastened on the sword over the tunic and tried walking around because he was not used to them. 'I cannot go in these,' he said to Saul, 'because I am not used to them.' So, he took them off." I realize that my armor may not work for everyone, like David using Saul's armor. But never bring a knife to a shoot-out. Make sure that you are spiritually armed and ready for battle when facing hardship. The enemy is determined, but as I have said before, "I was built for this!"

One day, my oncologist called to tell me he had heard

from the transplant team. I would need to see him in three months, then again in another three, to make sure everything was going well. He didn't know if I could get back on the list in the meantime. So, I called the transplant team and learned that, until I was fully cleared by the oncologist in six months, I would remain off the list.

I almost lost my way when I got that news. I had encouraged others not to schedule a time for your expectations of God, but once again, I was guilty of doing so. I had shown another moment of weakness in my expectations. I quickly let that go, understanding that I had to be more careful.

I asked my transplant coordinator some questions, hoping to feel some comfort. I wanted to know where I was on the list, and she told me I was in the high two-hundred range, but not to worry, I would not lose my place. I also learned it was not feasible to have potential donors begin the work-up process because their results may be too old by the time, we got to the transplant stage. I understood and I continued in my waiting season.

I never knew that I could wait like this. The old me was not built for this type of wait, but the new me considered this a test that I had to pass. I was really beginning to feel like Job. I had endured a great deal, but I could not give up. I had a few months until this was over.

While my restless leg syndrome continued to get worse, other medical conditions became concerning to the dialysis center staff. I knew that I was anemic, but my hemoglobin numbers had never dipped below 10, and now they had. I shared those lab results with the University of Illinois Hospital at my appointment the next day. They determined that my hemoglobin was low enough to require a blood transfusion, so I stayed overnight to receive it. They ran a test to find out why my hemoglobin was so low, but nothing was detected.

I had cleared my first post-radiation follow-up, and now I was dealing with this—another bump in the road. On top of that, my restless leg syndrome was getting progressively worse. I was not able to sleep at all in the evening. I took prescribed medication for it, I researched home remedies, a weighted blanket, I even started to walk around my bedroom at night, but nothing worked. I didn't know what else to do. This was a condition that many people knew nothing about. My doctors did not give me any additional remedies, so I continued to do the best I could to manage this issue—to no avail.

I did not want my chances to get back on the list to be affected by any other issues, so I remained focused and intentional about my health. The thing I was most happy with was that my gout had not reared its ugly head. There were days when I had some swelling in my lower extremities, but there was no gout pain. I had to celebrate the small victories.

I was still very aware of the enemy, but I felt that his attacks were losing steam. God was doing just what He said. I can say that I felt that I was fully relying on God; I was no longer trying to be in control. Alone, I was no match for Satan, but with God on my side, who could come against me?

I was preparing to have my last, six-month consultation regarding my radiation treatment. The oncologist wanted to check my PSA levels to measure my prostate's health. They also wanted to do an ultrasound. I scheduled the appointments and went in for the procedure. Soon after I got home, the call came.

My PSA levels were high. The cancer was back.

Chapter Fifteen

*"Therefore, if anyone is in Christ,
the new creation has come.
The old has gone, the new is here."*
– Corinthians 5:17

I began to pray. Again, I was seeking direction and answers. This was not supposed to be happening. I was doing all that I knew to do. Why was I being subjected to this disease all over again? I was a new creature. I had turned away from my old ways. My faith was beginning to wane.

"Abide in me, and I in you. As the branch cannot bear fruit of itself, except it abide in the vine, no more can ye, except ye abide in me. I am the vine, ye are the branches; He that abideth in me and I in him, the same bringeth forth much fruit for, without me, ye can do nothing" (John 15: 4-5). I knew that I did not have the answers, but the Holy Spirit reminded me that God does. He also reminded me that I can do nothing without God. I heard that message loud and clear. As quickly as my faith began to wane, I immediately came to my senses and recognized that God was my all and all. I had to reestablish my complete trust in God. James 1:5-6 says, "If you need wisdom, ask our generous God, and he will give it to you. He will not rebuke you for asking. But when you ask Him, be sure that your faith is in God alone. Do not waver, for a person with divided loyalty is as unsettled as a wave of the sea that is blown and tossed by the wind." I could not waver, nor could I be unsettled. I needed God now more than ever.

As I sat and continued to listen to the doctor, I learned that one of my kidneys had lesions on it and could be cancerous as well. As I began to digest all the information, I needed a moment. I prayed and let it all manifest into reality. At that moment, I was reminded of John 10:10: "The thief comes only to kill and steal and destroy; I have come that they might have life and have it to the full." This is the enemy's resume. He attempted to destroy my life, he attempted to steal my faith, and now, he was trying to kill me! I became incredibly angry. How dare he get so upset because of my faith and belief in God that he would actually try to kill me. As the doctor continued, in my mind, I decided to have a prostatectomy and a nephrectomy. These were surgeries that would remove both my prostate and the affected kidney. I shared this information with the doctor. I knew that these surgeries were necessary, and I was confident that God was my healer. I was not in this alone.

It was the winter of 2019, and I was looking forward to celebrating my birthday on January 2 in the new year, but I was anxious about my surgeries scheduled in April of 2020. The enemy was sure to keep me in a waiting season in the hope that he would break me. His attacks can come in a variety of ways. Physically, he attempts to ravish your body. Mentally, he pulls tricks and schemes to manipulate you. Spiritually, he literally tries to pull you away from God. He will use the very Word of God to trick you into doubting who God is. Matthew 4:6 says, "He will order His angels to protect you and they will hold you up with their hands, so you won't even hurt your foot on a stone." This was Satan's attempt to persuade Jesus into claiming a promise of God in a way it wasn't intended. A text out of context becomes a pretext.

The waiting season is where the enemy does some of his most effective work. It is important that, while you are still and focusing on the Word of God, you keep active in your thoughts and actions and use wisdom when you speak. Proverbs 16: 27-29 warn, "Idle hands are the devil's workshop; idle lips are his mouthpiece. An evil man sows strife: gossip separates the best of friends. Wickedness loves company and leads others into sin."

One of the most important things you can do in the waiting season is to perfect your ability to turn your cares and concerns over to God. Psalm 55:22 says, "Cast your cares on the Lord and He will sustain you; He will never let the righteous be shaken." If you achieve this, your mind and your spirit are free, and you can go forth and live your life without worry, fear, or doubt.

In this waiting season, I needed to be sustained. I will admit, my faith had been shaken, but I just kept my mind focused on Him. I was not about to give up. I don't believe He brought me this far to leave me. More than ever, I needed to call upon His promises and rest assured that He would be a promise keeper. Isaiah 55:11 says, "So is my word that goes out from my mouth. It will not return to me empty, but it will accomplish what I desire and achieve the purpose for which I sent it."

It is always good to reflect on your life to remind yourself of just how good He has been to you. I thought about how many people relied on the support group that I was facilitating. I thought about the work I had done over the last thirty years of my life. I began to understand that God had more for me to do now, I had to prepare; I knew that the work ahead of me was necessary. God had chosen me to be a leader and role model for thousands in my lifetime, and I could no longer take that for granted. I could not take full or partial credit for it—it was all God! God had done exceedingly and abundantly above all that I could have ever imagined. I began to feel better about myself. My faith that had been shaken was being restored. If He brought me through this before, He would do it again.

Throughout the last ten years, I had traveled over many peaks and valleys, and Satan had occupied space in my life for much of that time. Satan just would not take his hands off me. I held onto my gift of the Word of God, with Isaiah 54:17 in my spirit: "No weapon that is formed against me shall prosper."

I was preparing to turn fifty-eight years old. Growing older was a discouraging factor in the wait for a kidney transplant.

I continued to feel that the more I aged, the less likely I would be a prime candidate for a transplant. I cast those thoughts to the Lord, and I continued on. I made every effort to keep my mind on the goodness of God, but it was not easy for me. A word of advice: If you're struggling in your life or you feel as though your faith my not be where you want it to be, the answer is to pray. Remember all the good things He's done for you. If that doesn't work, recall all the blessings He has given to the important people in your life. You must find a way to keep your mind focused on the goodness of God and find your way back into the loving arms of the Lord.

The news of the cancer returning was a difficult pill to swallow. I had allowed my mind to turn to pessimistic thoughts, but I needed to keep my faith strong and not allow the thoughts and feelings I was having to consume me. I needed strength and courage. I needed God.

CHAPTER SIXTEEN

*"Do not grieve, for the joy of the Lord is your strength.
So do not fear, for I am with you;
do not be dismayed, for I am your God.
I will strengthen you and help you;
I will uphold you with my righteous right hand.
The Lord is my strength and my song;
he has given me victory."*
– Nehemiah 8:10

In 2020, I continued to struggle with restless leg syndrome. I was prescribed a new medication to no avail. Now, falling spells became an issue. Whenever I managed to fall asleep, I would fall out of my bed. The floor in the room where I stayed was tile with concrete underneath. This was extremely dangerous because my bed sits about two-and-a-half feet off the floor, so when I would fall it was not only painful, it was also potentially serious. My daughter and her husband went out and purchased me a bed rail. As much as I did not want to use a bed rail, I knew that I needed it and I greatly appreciated it. Although I felt like a child, I was able to swallow my pride and use it. Restless leg was once again disrupting things in my life. I was not resting at night. I wasn't able to stay awake during the day. I wasn't able to comfortably watch a television program because the sensation in my legs was so intense; standing was the only way to get some relief.

I am an avid football fan, so I look forward to the Super Bowl every year. Unfortunately, I knew that this year would be different because of my restless leg. Nevertheless, I was eagerly anticipating the contest. I am comfortable being alone most of the time, but the Super Bowl was a time for camaraderie and fellowship, and I felt that I needed that in this season. My nephew informed me that he and his wife were hosting a Super Bowl party. That was great news. It would keep my mind occupied, and I would get to talk football. I decided to attend the party on that Sunday. He didn't live far from me, so I figured that I could get there and back without the risk of exhaustion overcoming me during the drive. To ensure that I would be safe, I decided to have a female companion accompany me.

To deal with my restless leg, I decided that I would stand while watching the game. The women gathered upstairs to watch the game while the guys went to the basement. Every now and then, I went upstairs to check on my friend since she didn't really know anyone there, but she always looked comfortable.

I was hoping no one would notice that I was being severely challenged by my condition. I never took a seat, though there were seats available. The frequent trips upstairs really helped. Maybe people thought I was running to the restroom, but I had lost the ability to urinate some time ago. (This is quite common in dialysis patients.) It could have been that no one noticed anything at all, but I was aware, and I did not feel comfortable standing the entire time I was there nor taking frequent trips upstairs.

The game ended, and I rejoiced because the Chiefs won.

As we prepared to say our goodbyes, I began to feel tired. I wasn't drinking (I had given that up some time ago). I was exhausted from the restless leg and standing. I thought about asking my friend to drive, but my machismo prevented me from doing that; I felt I couldn't ask a lady to accompany me and then ask her to drive. So, we made our way to the car and began our return trip. It seemed as if we were caught by every red light. I felt myself dosing at a few of them. Although we were having conversations with the radio on, nothing was keeping me alert.

I felt cross-eyed. I began to pray that God would just get me home safely. That's all I wanted to do. I know, I know—I should have just asked her to drive. But there I was, trying to get us to my home where my companion's car was parked. As I approached the last traffic light, I began to thank God because, once again, He proved Himself as a protector. Although I was not home in the driveway, I knew that God would see this journey through to its completion. We continued talking about the game, and I felt like I got a second wind. I turned the next corner into my neighborhood. I was so glad to be home safely. I saw my companion off, and I went to my room to start my treatment and prepare for my night of challenging rest.

Chapter Seventeen

*"When I shut up the heavens so that there is no rain,
or command locusts to devour the land
or send a plague among my people, if my people,
who are called by my name, will humble themselves
and pray and seek my face and turn from their wicked ways,
then I will hear from heaven,
and I will forgive their sin and will heal their land."
– 2Chronicles 7:13-14*

I've often wondered whether God was really there for me, but in times of spiritual growth, those questions begin to diminish. The nights I made it home and wondered how I got there, the substances I consumed without being gravely damaged by them, the situations that I wanted but never had the opportunity to achieve—God was there the whole time. His ways are not our ways. Prayers are always answered, it's just that sometimes the answer is "no." I don't just recall the times when I got what I wanted; I also remember the times God kept me from dangers seen and not seen. God is awesome.

As the year rolled on, I began to anticipate the day of my surgeries. Although one kidney would be removed, my kidney problems were far from over as my remaining kidney was still dysfunctional. I was now fifty-eight years old, and I was approaching four years on dialysis. The month of April could not come soon enough.

February was an active month for me with doctor appointments, training assignments, the support group, and basketball games to keep my mind preoccupied. But I still had this restless leg issue to worry about. Even the rails on my bed couldn't stop me from falling while sitting or standing. Waiting grew more challenging. Just when I thought I had it under control, the restless leg added the weight of exhaustion while affecting my ability to wait in a fully conscious state.

Unbeknown to many, the falls were occurring more often. Some nights, I would just walk around my room until sunrise. If I had things scheduled, I would just power through them. I sought information about cannabis-based food products. I was very hesitant to pursue this avenue, but I felt that I was running out of options. I settled on the gummies with cannabidiol (CBD). I took two before bed and waited. After about an hour, nothing happened. I was not able to rest, and I didn't feel relaxed. I was told that I probably should have ordered the gummies with tetrahydrocannabinol (THC), but I decided not to. The restless leg syndrome continued. As I prepared for bed at night, instead of just walking around my room, I incorporated line dancing—specifically, the "Bus Stop." I would be up most of the night just dancing (to no music) until I would get tired. I would lie down for a moment, and when the restless leg started again, I would jump back up and begin to "Bus Stop" all over again. It was fun and entertaining but to no avail.

Coaching the basketball team was not a problem since I was up and active the entire time. Working was not an issue because I incorporated a great deal of interaction and movement into my sessions. The doctor appointments were another story. Doctor's offices have an area called "the waiting room." I didn't do well in the waiting rooms. I walked around a lot, I talked to other patients—I did things that were out of character for me. Several times, I caught myself drifting off so I would stand up and begin to pace the floor. I believe other patients wondered what was wrong with me. They probably thought I was worried about my appointment. I wasn't really sure, but I felt that I needed to do whatever it took to remain consciously aware of all that was happening around me. I did not want to fall to the floor in my doctor's office.

Before I knew it, February was over, and March was now upon me—my final hurdle. It was the turning point of my life.

As the month went on, we all began to hear about a virus that was sweeping the land.

My first thought was, "You have got to be kidding me!" We learned that this coronavirus, Covid-19, caused a variety of worrisome symptoms. We were now faced with a pandemic. I wanted answers—we all wanted answers—but in the beginning, there weren't many. So, I prayed, and I prayed, and I prayed! It sounded something like, "Lord, I really need you now (as if I didn't before). I don't know what to do (as if I did before). Lord, help me through this (as if He hadn't before)." It was my "back-against-the-wall-FOR-REAL" prayer. "By faith, the walls of Jericho fell, after the army had marched around them for several days" (Hebrews 11:30).

I was truly up against the wall, as I am sure many of you were. The world as we knew it had changed just as I was preparing to have the most important surgery of my life.

I thought about canceling the surgery, but the Holy Spirit continued to remind me to "do the work." But without the support I needed, how could I? I had come to rely on that so heavily in my life. And now, because of the pandemic, there would be no visitors allowed after my surgeries. All while I was having seizures and dealing with hypertension and gout, my support system was there. They helped to guide me through every situation. I was reminded of Psalms 55:22: "Cast thy burdens upon the Lord and He shall sustain. He shall never suffer thee." How quickly we forget. My Holy Spirit said to me, "Fully rely on God!" In that very moment of feeling the burden of the pandemic, I knew I had to search my heart. I thought that I was fully relying on God, but after further review, I wasn't. God wants complete and total surrender. I thought that I was a strong and self-sufficient person, but I was finding it difficult to fully surrender. What God showed me was my life as it was presently constructed.

My family was providing my shelter and a large part of my health care; I even needed their help with transportation. I was not independent—I just desired to be. I felt like He was saying to me, "You're already depending on others, why not fully rely on me?" It occurred to me once again that I needed to commit to God with my mind, body, and soul. I knew what I wanted, and He was the only one who was capable of giving me that and more.

Chapter Eighteen

*"Commit your way to the Lord;
trust in Him, and He will act."*
– Psalm 37:5

The pandemic's place in my journey was something I spent a great deal of time thinking about. Why was God allowing this if He says he would never forsake us? Deuteronomy 31:6 says, "Do not be afraid or terrified because of them for the Lord, your God, goes with you; He will never leave you nor forsake you." If God is allowing this, there must be a lesson to be learned. It wasn't long before I realized the answers were right there the whole time.

God wants us all to evolve—to grow spiritually. I felt that the more I was able to make sense of things going on in my life, the more settled and confident I became in my journey. I was able to see His purpose. I once heard someone say that faith was like walking up a flight of stairs without seeing the next step. I wanted to achieve unwavering faith, and I could have it if I fully committed to God.

On the day of my surgeries, I arrived at the University of Illinois Hospital. The procedures were vastly different from what I remembered. I was asked a series of questions and they checked my temperature before I could enter. Everyone was wearing masks; it looked like a scene from the movie Outbreak. After giving my thoughts and concerns to God, I was prepared to go into surgery.

I was groggy for two days after my surgery. I had no idea why I was responding that way. I was concerned and, once again, I wanted answers. Medical staff informed me that because of my renal failure, my body did not process the anesthesia normally. I was able to get through the first two days because I slept most of the time. The anesthesia was managing my restless leg. As I began to wake up, it started to dawn on me that I was not going to have any visitors; I would be there all alone. I spent most of my time in prayer, seeking God's protection and reassurance. I had made it through surgery. Recovery was the next step. This period of time made me stronger and much more confident in God. In the words of my pastor, I was "getting my faith up."

As I lay there in the hospital, I began to think about how different my life would be moving forward. Although my gout had become somewhat inactive, I was continuing to experience challenges with my restless leg. I thought about the effect that the pandemic was having. My church, like many others, began holding services virtually. In-person worship was not happening. My faith was strong, but I still had some adjusting to do. I really missed having physical access to my support system. I struggled during this waiting season.

Ephesians 2:8-10 says, "God saved you by his grace when you believed. And you can't take credit for this; it is a gift from God." Being reminded of this scripture provided me with some solace. I was growing spiritually and recognizing God's voice more frequently. I had learned so much from my personal experiences. The outside world had transitioned, and many things were different, but God remains the same—yesterday, today, and forevermore. The Holy Spirit continued to remind me of things I'd heard all my life but now, interpreted differently. The messages had so much relevance in my life, and I understood the necessity of recalling them and reflecting on them.

Chapter Nineteen

"For since the creation of the world, God's invisible qualities—his eternal power and divine nature—have been clearly seen, being understood from what has been made, so that people are without excuse."
– Romans 1:20

I was still struggling in my waiting season and eagerly awaited my discharge from the hospital. Soon, I was home with my support system. Things in the world were radically different and it required some adjusting. It was now the Spring of 2020 and summer was just around the corner. All church services were held virtually, as were my work assignments.

On Sunday mornings, I watched FMC's service on a variety of media outlets. I also observed other churches' virtual services. The levels of creativity I observed were encouraging. Ministries all over the country were tapping into new and creative ways to continue operations through the pandemic. This encouraged me. I also needed to become creative. I could not and would not allow this pandemic to negatively affect my journey. God was encouraging us to become new creatures while maintaining our faith and hope in Him.

I particularly focused on my church, FMC. There were churches losing members and some churches that even closed. While I believed that FMC would survive this pandemic, my concern was still there. I love my pastor and I know he is a Faith Mover, but this had to be troubling for him. I prayed often that God would encourage FMC and keep my pastor and his family strong and steady. Pastoring a church during the pandemic helped me to put things in perspective. Although I was being challenged with health issues, my pastor was responsible for the souls of thousands while maintaining the operations of a church facility. This was a challenging time for all. I knew that a sustained level of faith was important to my church as well as my health. I was determined to remain faithful.

Chapter Twenty

*"See, I am doing a new thing!
Now it springs up; do you not perceive it?
I am making a way in the wilderness
and the streams in the wasteland."*
– Isaiah 43:19

In the summer of 2020, the world's creativity was continuing to flourish. Drive-by celebrations, virtual meetings and graduations, online shopping, and more—people were adjusting. I, too, continued to adjust to this new season of my life. Now that the surgeries were behind me, I began to develop hope in my pursuit of receiving a new kidney.

Several weeks into my recovery, I noticed that I had some rectal bleeding. I tried not to be alarmed by this new development, but I must say, I was. I went to my dialysis clinic and told them about my bleeding issue, and they drew my labs and told me to monitor the bleeding, so that's what I did. Two days after my discussion with my dialysis nurse, I had a follow-up appointment at the University of Illinois Hospital.

On my way there, I received a call from my dialysis clinic. My nurse told me to hurry and get to an emergency room because my hemoglobin numbers had dropped to a dangerously low level. I informed her of where I was headed, and she urged me to go to their emergency room, so I did. I told them what my dialysis nurse had shared with me, and they immediately took my labs. When the results came back, the news was not good. They informed me that I needed a blood transfusion immediately and that they would have to admit me for further testing to find out why I was losing so much blood. I was numb. Here I was again, facing another medical challenge—during a pandemic, nonetheless. I was losing hope and I felt that I had taken all that I could take.

Chapter Twenty-One

"That was a turning point for many of the Jews who were with Mary. They saw what Jesus did, and believed in Him."
– John 11:45

I had given up. Not on God, but on myself. I knew that I could not continue to take part in this journey, not like I was. I held on to the fact that I was instrumental to this process. Of course, I believed in God, and yes, my faith had grown tremendously, but still, I had to be mindful of my thoughts and actions. I know that we must allow God into our lives, but for some reason, I was not giving Him the honor and respect He was due. It was truly in God's hands. Every time I think I've reached the level of faith that I wanted, revelation hits, I come back down to earth, and I realize that this is truly a journey and not a destination. Mental exhaustion, desperation, and confusion were occupying my life.

Although I had a colonoscopy recently, I was being asked to schedule another one. The thought of being back in the hospital during the pandemic was daunting. A couple of months after my discharge, I found myself back at the University of Illinois Hospital. This time, I took it like a champ. After spending a night in an emergency room, the attending physician came in to ask me a few questions. He then informed me that the nurses were striking, and they didn't have a room for me, so they were searching for another hospital to take me. The enemy was still busy. By disrupting my ability to have a room, he had effectively put me in another season of wait. I felt that he wanted to deny me my colonoscopy so that I would remain on dialysis forever. I was in a waiting season where my ability to actually "do something" was hampered by the fact that I was in this hospital but not yet admitted.

While waiting, I thought about the colonoscopy. The worst

part about the procedure was having to drink a gallon of disgusting fluid to clear the colon so the doctors have a better view. All the while, I continued to have a bleeding issue; I wondered if I would need another transfusion. But all I could do was wait! It was a major part of this journey.

I soon began to consider these moments not as seasons of waiting but as seasons of preparation. You can't have unwavering faith if you feel that you are waiting because waiting tends to come with weight. As I mentioned earlier, we must rebuke the weight that we put on ourselves. Preparation is the beginning stage of what's to come, and this was a revelation for me. This knowledge gave me a different perspective of what this season was really all about, even though I didn't know what I was preparing for—but I didn't have to know. All I knew was that God is the Head of my life. "But I would have you know that the head of every man is Christ...." (1Corinthians 11:3). Knowing that was enough for me.

After a nap and a dinner of soup and Jell-O, the nurse came into my room to inform me that I was being moved to Stroger Hospital, which was previously known as Cook County Hospital. Cook County Hospital was where I was born. Being a true child of God, I don't believe in coincidences; I believe they are messages from God. I wasn't quite sure what the message was, but I took this as a symbol of a clean slate and a fresh start. I believed that my past mistakes would be washed away, and I would move forward in confidence knowing God had forgiven me. 2Corinthians 5:17 says, "Therefore, if any man be in Christ, he is a new creature. Old things are passed away. Behold, all things become new." Inspired, I began to smile. Surrendering to Christ not only freed me of the weight and uncertainty, but it also gave me momentum. I was able to walk this journey with a feeling of liveliness. Everything was going to be okay.

My medical issues—the restless leg, what the colonoscopy might reveal, and the possible return of gout and seizures—

still caused me some concern. I also had noticed that I had physically transformed. My facial features changed because of a lack of rest and kidney failure. My skin had gotten darker, and the texture changed. There was no way I could manage it, so I just resigned myself to the fact that this was the new me. I didn't like it, but I couldn't allow it to affect my mind or spirit. I didn't look in mirrors very much because I didn't want to be reminded of how kidney disease had transformed my appearance. I knew that people would notice, but they were kind, and no one ever mentioned it to me. (That is, until much later. She knows who she is!) I knew that I was created in God's image, and that was the image I focused on. Given all that I had thought about and was currently faced with, I felt like a new man. The old man and the old thoughts were gone.

I arrived at Stroger with no fears, no concerns, and no worries—only a feeling of disgust when I thought about having to ingest that gallon of fluid. Nevertheless, I made myself comfortable in my room. Soon, a nurse entered my room with a gallon bottle of GoLytely. I looked at it on my food tray and turned away to watch television. Every so often, I would glance over at it, and to no surprise, it was still there. I grabbed the bottle and began to drink it. I had two hours to finish it. I wasn't allowed to eat or drink anything but GoLytely. As I continued my cleansing, I thought about the fact that I was closer to my goal of getting back on the list and hopefully receiving a kidney someday. I completed the cleanse, had the procedure, and prepared myself for what was next. I waited.

Chapter Twenty-Two

"Woe to the inhabiters of the earth and of the sea!
For the devil is come down unto you, having great wrath,
because he knoweth that he hath but a short time."
– Revelation 12:12

I waited for my results from my colonoscopy into the year 2021. On January 2nd, I celebrated my 59th birthday. I was approaching my five-year anniversary of being on dialysis. The month was busy with Zoom calls, training sessions, doctor appointments, and quality time with my three grandchildren. They may never know the motivation that their lives gave me. I knew I had to continue the fight. They are all so precious and I couldn't imagine not being part of their futures. I wanted to be here. They continue to be my inspiration. They give me a will and desire to go on. I love them dearly. I had to keep the Faith. I had to achieve victory!

When I was discharged from Stroger Hospital, the bleeding had stopped, and all that I needed were my results. A few days after my discharge, the nurse informed me that everything looked good! All they found were hemorrhoids. They removed some and performed rubber band ligation on the others. I was so excited by the great news, but I had to make sure those findings got over to the University of Illinois Hospital so I could get back on the kidney transplant list. I was in the high 200s when I was removed, and I never lost my place. I knew that I had to be closer to getting a transplant than I was before I was removed from the list.

I called my transplant team to give them the information, and they told me that they had to wait to receive the report from Stroger. I understood and prepared myself (waited) for the next step of the process. While I waited, the restless leg grew in intensity. I continued to have sleepless nights and terrifying, uncomfortable days. At least once a week, I fell out of the bed or out of my chair. Despite how terrified I was of the possibility of hurting myself, I held on to my faith and continued to do the work.

Several days had gone by and I had not heard from the medical center, so I called them. They informed me that the results of the procedure had not come to the hospital yet. So, I made another call to Stroger and learned that they were having trouble sending the report. I suggested that I could take the results over, but they declined. I was really trying to put this piece of the puzzle behind me. If I needed to get involved, I was willing to do it. A few days letter, Stroger informed me that the results had been delivered. Yes! Now I was preparing (waiting) for the news from my transplant team. I called them and found out that they were not in possession of the results, but that they were waiting to receive information from the colorectal team before they could make any decisions. While they were waiting, I was waiting (preparing). When was this ride going to end? All I could do was continue to believe in God and trust that everything was in order and designed just the way He intended. Many times I wished that I knew His way and His plans. Luke 22:42 says, "Father, if You are willing, remove this cup from me. Yet not my will, but Your will be done." Even Jesus had a moment when He didn't want to face the cross. He quickly recalled the level of faith He had in His Father's word, and He retracted His request. I found comfort in knowing that, and I continued to wait (prepare).

While in this season of waiting, I did some work on my computer. While sitting there, I began to feel sleepy. I nodded off a couple of times, and I decided to abandon the work and prepare myself for bed. The last thing I wanted to do was fall again. I got up and sat on the side of my bed. I became interested in what was on the television as I removed my shoes. I went to remove my socks, but the next thing I remember was picking myself up off the floor. I immediately reached for my forehead because I was in pain. I feared that there would be blood, but there was no blood. I gathered myself and headed for the bathroom to see what was causing the pain. Apparently, I had fallen onto the floor headfirst. When I looked in the mirror, there was a huge lump on the left side of my head. I immediately called my daughter, and she came and examined me. After her examination, we headed to the hospital again. This time, we went to Community Hospital in Munster, Indiana. It was closer and I had been there previously when I had my peritoneal infection.

I checked in at the front desk and was immediately taken to the back. They asked questions, did a CT scan, and then, you guessed it, I waited. I thought about the fact that Satan was not going to stop. He was determined to end my life, one way or another. I was pacing up and down the hospital corridor. Not because I was worried, but because I didn't want to sit down and fall asleep. I chuckled when I thought of all the attempts Satan had made; hypertension, gout, multiple seizures, renal failure, dialysis, infection, restless leg syndrome (and all that came with it), cancer (not once, but twice), rectal bleeding, and now this. Through it all, I was still standing—standing firm in the belief and knowledge of God. I couldn't imagine that he would have more attacks coming, but the enemy is a determined foe. In that moment, I knew that God was with me and that He was my protection. I was as confident as ever. I began to thank the Lord.

Satan, you cannot win!

Chapter Twenty-Three

*"For I am about to do something new.
See, I have already begun. Do you not see it?
I will make a pathway through the wilderness.
I will create rivers in the dry wasteland."*
– Isaiah 43:19

My results came back, and everything was fine. I was released and allowed to go home. While I enjoyed a sense of relief, I prepared myself for what was to come. I was still waiting to hear back from the hospital regarding my colonoscopy results. At the time, I wasn't even thinking about getting a transplant, nor was I thinking about getting back on the list. I just settled in and allowed God to be God. All along this journey, I never felt this level of calmness in my spirit. I'd like to tell you that it was a conscious effort on my part—I really would—but that calmness came from God.

The next day, the University of Illinois Hospital called. They informed me that the results from my colonoscopy were not clear enough. They wanted me to have another—two colonoscopies within two months. They told me that they would call me when it was scheduled. So, I waited for their call.

On the morning of March 8th, I received a call. I answered and calmly prepared myself for what they were going to tell me. The woman on the line was not calling from the colorectal team. She was my transplant coordinator. They had received all the information from my doctors, and they were going to meet the upcoming Friday to review my case to determine my status on the transplant list. This was unexpected news, but it was nothing to get too excited about. Especially with the impending colonoscopy procedure, I could not get prematurely optimistic. After our brief conversation, I began to pray and reflect. I prayed for strength and focus. I was content and I was not going to be thrown off.

One of the most powerful and impactful things I experienced on this journey was the pandemic. I didn't realize how much I would miss attending church. The wonderful thing about my pastor is his faith. He genuinely believes that prayer changes things. So, while our church was closed, that's what we did as a congregation...WE PRAYED. Every morning at seven o'clock, we would call into the prayer line and one of the ministry staff would pray. They typically had a specific focus like community, health, finances, etc. I looked forward to those calls because they helped me start my day, and they helped me to keep my mind focused on God. One day after the prayer call, my phone rang. It was the nurse from my dialysis center informing me that I could get the vaccine that day, March 12, 2021. I felt like I was one step closer to victory over this season of my journey. Because I got the Moderna vaccine, which requires two shots, I had to wait until April 9th to be fully vaccinated. That was fine with me; I was in a season of wait (preparation) anyway.

I was approaching five years of dialysis. One of the most tedious aspects of dialysis was when I traveled. I took my dialysis machine with me, and I needed to call my dialysis materials supplier and have them ship supplies to my destination. When I arrived at my hotel, I had several boxes of supplies waiting for me. All my travel was business-related, which made traveling more challenging because I was on a schedule. My brother-in-law usually traveled with me, which was a tremendous help.

I felt that I made the adjustments to accept things as they were, and I continued to do the work. I had a fairly good life. It was not the way I would've designed it, but I was not the architect—God was. The journey would continue. I just needed to lean on my support and embrace all the goodness surrounding me. The enemy was going to do what he was going to do. I just needed to let God be God.

Chapter Twenty-Four

*"Call to me and I will answer you and tell you
great and unsearchable things you do not know."*
– Jeremiah 33:3

I didn't want to go through another colonoscopy, but if it was God's will, then so be it. Surrendering to God provided me with so much peace on my journey. I didn't think about what was to come or what I wanted to come; I just went about living my life as it was presently constructed. Jeremiah 3:16 says, "And when your land is once more filled with people, says the Lord, you will no longer wish for the good old days." I can honestly say that the old me was gone. I did not want the old me and I did not like the old me. However, I appreciated the old me because I learned some critical lessons. Although there were things I would change in my life, I wouldn't change my level of faith. I genuinely love God and am committed to serving him. I just understood that I had done all that I could do and there was nothing else left for me to do but glorify and worship him.

They were set to review my case on March 12th, and as I expected, I didn't get a call that day with any news. I had endured this journey for 5 years; I was prepared to wait as long as I needed to. I was now waiting on God. So, I spent that day with my three grandchildren. I loved watching them play together. Oftentimes, I would give them my telephone to play with. Usually, when I gave them my phone, I never knew how it might return to me. The lighting of the screen or size of the font might be different, or they might have made a call. Because these were my grandchildren, I didn't care. I just wanted them to be happy. I was happy because I got to spend the weekend with them. Unbeknown to me, there was a change to my phone that I was not aware of until a few days later. They had silenced my ringer. Although I wasn't thinking about the transplant team call, I would've missed their call anyway. Psalm 31:15 says, "My future is in your hands. Rescue me from those who hunt me down relentlessly." Satan was definitely doing that, but his reign of terror was coming to an end.

On March 14th, I began my day on the prayer call, as I usually would. After the call, I went about my day by managing the restless leg and waiting for either the colorectal team or the transplant team to call. Neither did. Later that day, I was on the phone with a friend of mine and my phone clicked. It was the hospital calling—not the colorectal team but the transplant team, and on a Sunday evening. They told me I was back on the list, a candidate for a transplant. How could that be? I know that the colonoscopy they received from Stroger was not clear, so how was this possible? I stopped questioning it and just allowed God to be God. The Holy Spirit quickly reminded me of Jeremiah 29:11: "For I know the plans I have for you...." I didn't need to know because this was God moving and speaking.

The next two days came and went with no call from colorectal—the only call I anticipated. The transplant team had just given me great news, but I was clear about the transplant process: It could take months, even years, but HALLELUJAH, I was glad to be back on the list! This colorectal request was sent to disrupt my season of waiting, but I didn't allow it. I had taken my hands off it and allowed God to be God.

The day was Wednesday, March 17th. As usual, I started my day with my prayer call. This particular day the person praying was my pastor's wife, The First Lady. I know I haven't mentioned her up until now, but as you know, behind every great man is the strength of a great woman supporting him. I loved when our First Lady prayed because there was a fire and an anointing in her words and delivery that made you feel you were going to be victorious. She started the call with updates and announcements. At that moment, my phone clicked. I did not want to miss her prayer, but when I looked at the call, I saw it was the hospital. What was Satan up to now? He knows how much I love when my First Lady prays, so that's when he sent in the colorectal team. It was seven o'clock in the morning; I couldn't imagine why they would be calling me so early. Had they scheduled a procedure for that day? I almost didn't answer, but I did.

"Mr. Baugh, we may have a kidney for you"

If I were not on that prayer call, I would have missed this call!

I was in shock. I was put back on the list only three days ago. How was this possible?

She went on to inform me that I was third on the list. Although I might not get a call that day, she wanted me to be ready just in case. She said that they would know by five o'clock because a family had decided to end efforts to prolong the life of the donor.

In biblical terminology, three represents the harmony of God's presence: The Trinity, three days until the resurrection, my three grandchildren, my position on the transplant list, and receiving this news three days after getting back on the list. This was no coincidence. Clearly, this was evidence of God moving and speaking.

I concluded the call and clicked over. Our First Lady had begun her prayer, and when I rejoined the call, the first words that I heard her say were, "Something good is going to happen to you today!" If I had any doubt, there was my confirmation! I was getting a kidney today! I knew it, and I stood on it. As I prepared myself for the call for my transplant, I checked my phone to make sure that my ringer was on and the volume was turned up. That is when I realized that my grandchildren had turned my ringer off days before the call came, a few days before the call notifying me that I was back on the list. But I had surrendered, and God was in full control. There was a boldness and assurance that came over me, so much so that I packed my bag in preparation for my hospital stay. I knew that I was going to the hospital and that I would be there for several days. I began to inform some friends and family to tell them of the upcoming event, and here are some of the responses I got: "Don't get your hopes up," "You are number three, maybe it'll happen this summer," "Just wait and see what happens at five o'clock," and my favorite, "The family may change their minds." They were all legitimate, caring concerns, and I love the people that offered those words. Thank you all, but I was now operating with unwavering faith. My pastor had always encouraged us to "get our faith up." Well, mine was extremely high because I had heard from the Lord Himself. There was nothing that anyone could do or say to deter me.

I sat in my room in silence. A couple of people joined me, but I was not wavering or bending. God had transformed my five-year struggle into a three-day miracle. I reflected on how God strategically removed, arranged, and placed people in my life to get me to my eagerly anticipated end. He is so amazing; I cannot praise Him enough. So, I waited—continued to wait on God.

At about 2:30 in the afternoon, I received a call informing me that without a fresh blood draw, they may have to skip over me. I told her I would be right there. God spoke this and orchestrated it. I was not about to give Satan the victory of blocking this blessing. My brother and I jumped in his car and drove the 30 miles to the University of Illinois Hospital. I gave them blood, jumped back in the car, returned home, and continued to wait. This season of wait was different than any I had experienced before. I had completely surrendered to God—He was in full control. As we waited, the five o'clock hour was approaching. 2Peter 3:6 says, "But you must not forget this one thing, dear friends: A day is like a thousand years to the Lord, and a thousand years is like a day to the Lord."

Five o'clock came and went without a call, so I continued to wait. I knew that there was the colonoscopy still not scheduled and I knew that it was beyond the final hour they spoke of, but I had faith in the Divine God that I vowed to serve. There was no more weight; I had victory over that. I was comfortable and content waiting. It was around seven o'clock when a call came. The person on the other end said, "Mr. Baugh, how soon can you get here?" This was it! I was going to have my transplant. As I exited my home, my former pastor prayed over me, and the house was erupting with joy and reverence of God. I remained calm as I got in the car with my brother. The calm and serenity God had allowed me to adopt gave me the assurance that He was going to do just what He said! I just didn't know how fast He would.

I was soon at the hospital, prepped and ready for surgery. They put a mask on my face, and the next thing I knew, I was awake in a room with a new kidney. With the virus becoming more contained, the hospital adjusted the restrictions and allowed a single visitor per day. When I came to my room, my oldest daughter was there. I could barely talk but rejoicing and praising God was the order of the day. My complete surrender was necessary for me to receive what God had for me.

I continue to thank God for being patient with me and sticking by me. I endured these last ten years, and I am a changed person because of it. I figure if God waited on me through all my misgivings, mistakes, and poor decisions, the least I could do was to learn how to wait on Him. This journey was long and sometimes difficult but, in the end, I achieved victory! Victory in the wait.

Go Forth in Victory

The journey to unwavering faith will look different for everyone. Unwavering faith is something that many of us find difficult to achieve. Faith is trust, belief, and confidence that what you are hoping for will come to pass. When your faith is rooted and firmly planted in God, just like the smallest seed on Earth, it grows in size and in strength. Investing in your level of faith increases optimism while diminishing pessimism. The world constantly challenges our faith. Fear, doubt, and anger are just some of the ways we know our faith is in jeopardy, but the world accepts those emotions. I know that was my experience. Although the journey might be different, the basic ingredients of unwavering faith are the same.

There were many aspects of this journey I would like to revisit to help you understand how God is and where I am during the time of this publication.

- My Divorce: My ex-wife (LaWanda) and I remain close friends. She has moved away and started a new life. I wish things had worked out differently, but I guess it was not to be. His ways are not our ways; His thoughts are not our thoughts. I don't know what God has in store for us, but I will continue to trust in Him.

- FMC: I am still a member of FMC, and we are still standing strong. Our outreach is as great as it's always been, and we are in a season of a "Got Jesus?" campaign. God is saving souls, and I am continuing to grow in faith. Our pastor and First Lady (Moses B. and LaCresha Herring) are still operating in faith. Website: faithmoverschurch.org   to find out more.

- Other relationships: My crew has greatly diminished.

I still stay in touch with some by phone, but I don't interact with them. I've given my new crew a new name: "family." My dialysis nurse (Laura Shaw-Kubica) and I are still friends, and I visit her at the center every few weeks. I've reconnected with some lifelong friends and established some new and meaningful relationships. Stay tuned.

- Illnesses: Since I received "Kid Kidney," my blood pressure medications have decreased in number and dosage. My blood pressure has been regulated. I have not experienced any gout symptoms. I have been taken off anti-seizure medication and was informed by my neurologist that there was no sign of potential seizure activity. The impending colonoscopy was put on hold indefinitely due to medical staffing. Lastly, my restless leg syndrome is no more! It stopped a few days after my transplant. All signs are pointing towards complete restoration.

- Arrangements: I am still with my sister and brother-in-law/former pastor (Juanita and Reverend Anthony Lowe)

- My children, Kayla (Mario), Takiya and grandchildren (Leilani, Linae, and Leah) are well. I continue to embrace my support system, and they continue to be there for me.

Achieving Unwavering Faith

- Romans 10:17: "Consequently, faith comes from hearing the message, and the message is heard through the word about Christ." It is important that you become part of a Bible-centered preaching and teaching ministry. Find someone who will rightly divide the word of truth.

- 1John 3:6: "No one who abides in Him keeps on sinning; no one who keeps on sinning has either seen Him or known Him." It is essential that you genuinely know and believe in God. You need a relationship with Him through a fervent and consistent prayer life and reading and understanding His word.

- Lamentations 3:25-26: "The Lord is good to those whose hope is in Him, to the one who seeks Him. It is good to wait quietly for the salvation of the Lord." Learn how to wait. Be sure that your waiting doesn't come with weight. Focus on the goodness of God and not on what you don't have. Be still and know that He is God.

- 2Corinthians 5:17: "Therefore, if anyone is in Christ, the new creation has come." Release the old you. I know this can be challenging, but you can't put old wine into new wineskins. Embrace the new you and resist the temptation to re-establish the old.

- Ephesians 6:11: "Put on the full armor of God, so that you can stand against the devil's schemes. Be fully dressed: The enemy is going to be persistent. You must prepare for battle. He is the great tempter. Stand strong and resist his attacks. YOU were built for this!

- Romans 12:3: "For by the grace given me, I say unto you: Do not think of yourself more highly than you ought, but rather think of yourself with sober judgment, in accordance with the measure of faith God has given you." This journey is not a sprint, it's a marathon. Expect God to do what He said without putting an expectation of time on God.

- Matthew 4:4: "Jesus answered, 'It is written: Man shall not live on bread alone, but on every word that comes from the mouth of God.'" Declare His promises and speak God's word. It builds you up and keeps you reminded of what God has done.

- John 8:47: "Whoever belongs to God says, 'The reason you don't hear is that you do not belong to God.'" Learn to listen to God. Listening to and hearing from God is somewhat like learning a new language. You must be intentional about it. You must surrender to Him to hear from Him.

- Nehemiah 8:10: "And Nehemiah continued, 'Go feast of rich foods and sweet drinks and share gifts of food with people who have nothing prepared. This is a sacred day before our Lord. Don't be dejected and sad, for the joy of the Lord is your strength!'" Whatever you are going through or whatever you are facing, know that the joy of the Lord is your strength. You are alive and God is with you. Live with joy. No one said it would be easy, but the Bible says all things are possible with God.

I pray that all who read this will understand the importance of how you wait. God has a plan for our lives, and we demonstrate our trust and belief in His plan by how we wait. Learn to avoid the weight during your season of wait. Hebrews 12:1 says, "Therefore, since we are surrounded by such a huge crowd of witnesses to the life of Faith, let us strip off every weight that slows us down, especially the sin that so easily trips us up. And let us run with endurance the race God has set before us."

Embrace your seasons of wait. It is an opportunity for us to show God just how much we love Him and believe in His word. God has truly been gracious and kind to me, and I now understand the importance of knowing how to wait in order to achieve victory.

I made many mistakes and lost many people and things I felt were important to me. Knowing that God has a plan for my life, I will continue to work to sustain the level of faith I have achieved. God's word never returns to Him void. God is able to do exceedingly and abundantly above all you could ever ask or think. Ask it in faith and you shall receive it. I am a living witness.

Wait, I say, on the Lord.

BIBLE STUDY QUESTIONS

Chapter One
- What does Psalm 27:14 mean? What does it mean to "be in good courage?"
- What does Hebrews 11:6 suggest?

Chapter Two
- If planning is important, what is Proverbs 16:9 saying?
- What should we be doing if God directs our footsteps?
- What does Hebrews 11:1 mean?

Chapter Three
- What does it mean to "Be still" in Psalm 46:10?
- What does it mean when the author writes, "His thoughts are not our thoughts; our ways are not His ways"?
- "With men, this is impossible; but with God, all things are possible" (Matthew 19:26). What does this mean?

Chapter Four
- Ephesians 6:14-17 describes a wardrobe. Why is this wardrobe important?
- How did the absence of this wardrobe affect the author in Chapter Four?
- What does the author mean by, "There are going to be some things you must release in order for you to receive what God has for you"?

Chapter Five
- In Job 2:6, why did God allow Satan access to Job?
- In John 1:9, why is it important that we "confess our

sins?"
- Psalm 46:1 says, "God is our refuge." Where else might people find a hiding place?

Chapter Six

- In 1Corinthians 15:58, what does "be steadfast and unmovable, always abounding in the work of the Lord" mean?
- Galatians 6:7 says, "Do not be deceived: God cannot be mocked. A man reaps what he sows." What does this scripture mean?
- Proverbs 3:5 says, "Trust in the Lord with all your heart and lean not on your own understanding." What does the scripture encourage?

Chapter Seven

- What does 1Corinthians 10:13 mean and what are examples of this meaning?
- Is Psalm 23:4 a contradiction to God directing our steps? If so, how? If not, explain?
- What was happening in the author's life to lead him to repeat Isaiah 54:17: "No weapon formed against thee shall prosper"?

Chapter Eight

- In this chapter, explain the author's feelings and how they were necessary to his journey to unwavering faith.
- What did the author mean when he said, "I could hear God saying, "'My word never returns to me void'"?
- Psalms 12:13 says, "He will not let your foot slip. He who watches over you, He will not slumber." What does this scripture mean?

Chapter Nine

- 2Corinthians 10:3-4 says, "For though we walk in the flesh, we do not war after the flesh. For our weapons of our warfare are not carnal, but mighty through God to the pulling down of strongholds." What does this scripture mean, and how did it relate to the author's journey?
- John 14:26 states, "But I will leave you a comforter, which is the Holy Ghost, whom the Father will send in my name, he shall teach you all things, and bring all things to your remembrance, whatsoever I have said unto you." Why is this scripture important, and how do we access the Holy Spirit?
- Deuteronomy 31:6 says, "Be strong and courageous. Do not be afraid or terrified because of them, for the Lord your God goes with you, He will never leave you nor forsake you." Have you ever been in fear? If so, why were you not able to cling to this scripture?

Chapter Ten

- Proverbs 28:1 states, "The wicked flee when no one pursues, but the righteous are bold as a lion." How did this scripture relate to the author's journey?
- Why did the author say, "I see you Satan, and no weapon formed against me shall prosper"? Where in the bible can you find something similar to this?
- Scripturally, why was the author continuing to go through more challenges?

Chapter Eleven

- Lamentations 3: 56-57 says, "You heard my plea. Do not close your ears to my cry for relief. You came near when I called you and you said, do not fear." What was the scripture displaying?
- Job 7:11-12 (NIV) says, "Therefore I will not keep silent. I

will speak out in the anguish of my spirit; I will complain in the bitterness of my soul." Why was this important to Job, and why would the author reference this at that point of his journey?
- John 8:24 says, "Unless you believe that I am who I claim to be, you will die in your sins." What does this scripture mean?

Chapter Twelve

- Matthew 6:6 says, "But when you pray, go into your room, close your door, and pray to your father, who is unseen. Then your father, who sees what is done in secret, will reward you." Why is this scripture important, and was the author able to do this?
- Philippians 4:6 states, "Do not be anxious about anything but in every situation, by prayer and petition, with thanksgiving present your request to God." Do you find this difficult? Why is this scripture important to the author's journey?
- The author spoke these words, "When my treatment ended, the Holy Spirit reminded me of the many blessings I had experienced in the last few years." Do you think remembering is important? Why or why not?

Chapter Thirteen

- Habakkuk 2:3 states, "For still the vision awaits its appointed time, it hastens to the end—it will not lie. If it seems slow, wait for it, it will surely come; it will not delay." What does this scripture mean?
- Why do you think God was attacking the author in his body?
- Why was it important that the author remained faithful and reflected?

Chapter Fourteen

- What does the Bible mean when it says, "There is no condemnation," in Romans 8:1?
- In 1Samuel 17:38-39, what was the author trying to illustrate as it relates to his journey?
- Why would the author say that he "felt like Job"?

Chapter Fifteen

- What does John 15: 4-5 mean? What fruit is it referencing?
- How does James 1:5-6 relate to this part of the author's journey?
- Was there a time when Proverbs 16: 27-29 was relevant in your life?

Chapter Sixteen

- Do you feel that the author was allowing Nehemiah 8-10 to get in his spirit at this time of his journey?
- Do you think that the author should've been praying for something more than just getting home?

Chapter Seventeen

- What does 2Chronicles 7:13-14 mean to you?
- Hebrews 11: 30 states, "By faith, the walls of Jericho fell, after the army had marched around them for several days." What was happening at the time of this scripture?
- Psalms 55:22 says, "Cast thy burdens upon the Lord, and He shall sustain: He shall never suffer thee." Why is this sometimes difficult to do?

Chapter Eighteen

- Deuteronomy 31:6 says, "Do not be afraid or terrified because of them, for the Lord, your God goes with you;

He will never leave you nor forsake you." Who is this scripture referring to when it says "them"?
- In Ephesians 2:8 and 10, what is meant by "Grace" and "Gift?"
- What does the author mean when he says "recognizing God's voice more"?

Chapter Nineteen
- Romans 1:20 states, "For since the creation of the world God's invisible qualities, his eternal power and divine nature have been clearly seen, being understood from what has been made, so that people are without excuse." What does this scripture mean?
- How does this scripture relate to this chapter?

Chapter Twenty
- In Isaiah 43:19, what does it mean when the writer says "a way in the wilderness and the streams in the wasteland"?
- In your opinion, why was the author giving up hope, and what scripture would you encourage him to read in this moment?

Chapter Twenty-One
- What scripture describes a person that gives up on themselves but continues to believe in God?
- Does the author's comparison of waiting versus preparing make sense? Why or why not?
- What does 2Corinthians 5:17 mean?

Chapter Twenty-Two
- Revelation 12:12, "Woe to the inhabiters of the earth and of the sea! For the devil is come down unto you, having

great wrath, because he knoweth that he hath but a short time." What does this scripture mean?
- Luke 22:42 says, "Father, if You are willing, remove this cup from me. Yet not my will, but Your will be done." What was going on with the author that relates to this scripture?

Chapter Twenty-Three
- Why was the author's ability to attend his church so important? Can you identify a scripture to support your answer?
- The author said that the pandemic had the biggest impact on him. Do you feel that Sin is a pandemic?

Chapter Twenty-Four
- Jeremiah 3:16 states, "And when your land is once more filled with people, says the Lord, you will no longer wish for the good old days." How does this scripture relate to the author's journey at this time?
- Psalm 31:15 says, "My future is in your hands. Rescue me from those who hunt me down relentlessly." What was going on in the scripture and how does it relate to the author's situation in his life?
- 2Peter 3:6 says, "But you must not forget this one thing, dear friends; A Day is like a thousand years to the Lord, and a thousand years is like a day to the Lord." What does this scripture mean?

www.ingramcontent.com/pod-product-compliance
Lightning Source LLC
Chambersburg PA
CBHW030451010526
44118CB00011B/886